# welcome to

# THE KOP ANNUAL 2011

TOM and George might not be welcome here, but Kopites most certainly are and after the year Liverpool FC have had we could all do with cheering up.

That's what The Kop Annual 2011 is all about – having a laugh.

We're absolutely convinced this year's offering will make you chuckle and we promise to have a joke in the Kop Annual within 60 pages.

This is the magnificent 7th Kop Annual we have produced and it is the most environmentally friendly yet as we significantly cut carbon emissions by deciding not to travel to any Champions League games in 2010.

If Liverpool's start to the season under Roy Hodgson is anything to go by then we'll be adopting a similar policy for the Europa League in 2011…and the Premier League in 2011/12.

All the talk might be about American takeovers, but with Hodgson, Martin Broughton, Joe Cole, Glen Johnson, Paul Konchesky and Jonjo Shelvey all knocking about the place, there has already been a Cockney takeover at Anfield.

With Roy also narrowly missing out on adding Carlton Cole to his squad, we decided an East-end theme was appropriate for the front of The Kop Annual 2011. Sick, innit?

Of course you might be a Kop Annual newbie, someone unfortunate enough not to have discover us until now, so we should really explain who we are.

The Kop Annual is produced by the makers of The Kop Magazine – a monthly Liverpool FC publication that combines humour with serious comment and in-depth analysis with scandalous gossip.

We also have a Twitter page – @TheKopMagazine – that has more followers than Steven Gerrard and Fernando Torres put together, although that could change if they join Twitter.

Every year we take The Kop's best bits and mix them with a load of brand new features to compile the 84-page glossy publication you now have in your hands.

This year you'll find a Welcome to the Kop Annual 2011 article on page four which tells you exactly what is in the Kop Annual 2011, including a Welcome to the Kop Annual 2011 article on page four that welcomes you to the Kop Annual 2011.

Kop Karaoke is always popular so we've penned three brand new tunes – including Alicia Keys' Geordie State of Mind – while Ashley Cole stars in the Ex-Factor and there's all of PAK's (Peter King) iconic Kop cartoons.

We bring you the true story behind Carra's World Cup and ask 'who's hairline is it anyway?' in our exclusive quiz that tests if you can tell the difference between Pepe Reina's head and Jordan's tits.

The story behind the chants gives a somewhat surprising insight into the real origins of many Kop songs, we focus on the Newton Heath Supporters Union, Spirit of Docherty (SOD), and publish the best Spotteds and Kop Summer Challenge 5 snaps of the year.

Annual favourites such as You Ask, We Answer and LFC Bay are here as usual and we've got plenty of Kop Mole titbits, Ryan Babel tweets, Kop classifieds and digs at Everton, Chavski and Newton Heath to keep you entertained.

So welcome to the Kop Annual 2011 and if we don't make you laugh then check out our special money-back guarantee on page 85.

Photographic credits: Trinity Mirror, PA Pics. Illustrations: Peter King.
Writing: Chris McLoughlin. Design/editing: Lee Ashun, Paul Dove, Roy Gilfoyle, Michael McGuinness, Adam Oldfield, Barry Parker

At least some of our players won something in 2010... in July a crocked Fernando Torres and croaky Pepe Reina (after his microphone shenanigans) returned from the World Cup victorious and had a new manager in Roy Hodgson waiting for them

# THE BOSS'S BIG MOVE UP NORTH

They say moving home is one of the most stressful things you can do in life, especially if you're making a big step like relocating from London to Liverpool (and taking on a stressful job where the company owners are causing trouble...) The Kop Annual followed Roy Hodgson as he arrived on Merseyside

*Hmmmm... maybe I should rent the old place for a bit in case I need to pop back*

SOLD
1 COCKNEY MANSION

**After stepping off the train and shopping in Liverpool One (Everton Nil), Roy finally got a few hours to take a look at his new home**

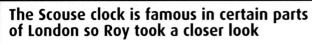

*The Boat Race is a bit different in Liverpool...*

**The Scouse clock is famous in certain parts of London so Roy took a closer look**

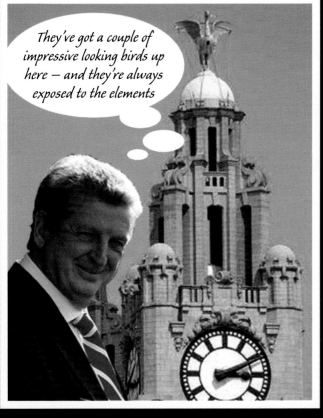

*They've got a couple of impressive looking birds up here – and they're always exposed to the elements*

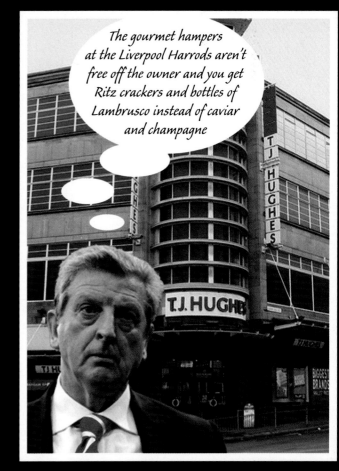

*The gourmet hampers at the Liverpool Harrods aren't free off the owner and you get Ritz crackers and bottles of Lambrusco instead of caviar and champagne*

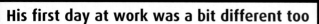

I've brought up a mate to make me feel at home — but he got into a bit of trouble so I didn't see him for a while

But Roy soon got used to Liverpool and he was given a warm welcome by everyone. The only problem was he soon discovered that his work colleagues just weren't producing the goods which made his life very difficult...

To be continued...

# ROONEY'S ESCORTS

**Looking for a new ride? Want to get your motor running with a different model? I'm your man.**

## ESCORT #1

### £35

This original model comes at a knocking good shop price and is ideal for first-time drivers down to their last bit of brass. It'll get you from A to B quickly, although maybe a little too quickly.

## ESCORT #2

### £45

This auld banger really goes when you put a bit of fuel into the tank. It's seen better days, and won't be to everyone's tastes, but I've been in it myself in Liverpool and it certainly goes like the clappers.

## ESCORT #3

### £1,200

There's only one way of describing the Jen-erous price of this sexy little number – juicy! Made in Bolton, it's the ideal model for anyone looking for a regular ride and many of my footy friends have test-driven it.

## ESCORT #4

### £3,333

Already bought a couple of escorts? Why not have a threesome by getting your hands on my latest model? Get spotted in this and it'll definitely make the papers. Buy it? Helen would.

**ROONEY MOTORS**

**SPECIALIST IN ESCORTS**

When Stevie's model made it into Madame Tussaud's in 2010, we updated you with the latest wax stories to hit the headlines

# YOU'LL NEVER WALK A CLONE

## WAXING LYRICAL – ALL YOUR LATEST WAX RELATED NEWS

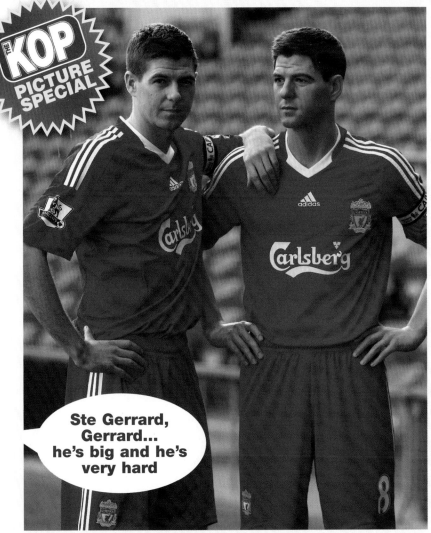

**THE KOP PICTURE SPECIAL**

Ste Gerrard, Gerrard... he's big and he's very hard

There's only one Steven Gerrard...at least there was until Madame Tussauds unveiled their new waxwork

■ **Manchester City have been linked with a £60 million move for Steven Gerrard's waxwork**

■ *Alan Hansen asked Gary Lineker to unblock his ears so Tussauds can build a team of Carraghers next*

■ *John Terry has asked Madame Tussauds to create a waxwork of him that he can leave at home with the wife while he's playing away*

■ *Rafa Benitez admitted that the Steven Gerrard waxwork is ahead of Alberto Aquilani in the midfield pecking order but not Lucas and Fabio Aurelio as he likes a full Brazilian down the middle*

■ *Share prices in wax-making companies reached an all-time high following rumours that Madame Tussauds were thinking of buying enough wax to make Frank Lampard*

■ *Steven Gerrard is the first Scouse dummy to be seen wearing a Liverpool shirt since Jason McAteer*

■ *Liverpool were in for a waxwork of Philipp Degen to see if it can stay in position better than the real thing*

# whose hairline is it anyway?

IT WAS ONCE PERMS AND TASHES BUT NOW IT'S A WHOLE NEW BALD GAME AS THE REDS PLAY IT SHORT. BUT CAN YOU TELL YOUR KONCHESKYS FROM YOUR KOJAKS? TRY OUR PICTURE QUIZ TO SEE IF YOU'RE THE CREAM OF THE CROP...

**1**

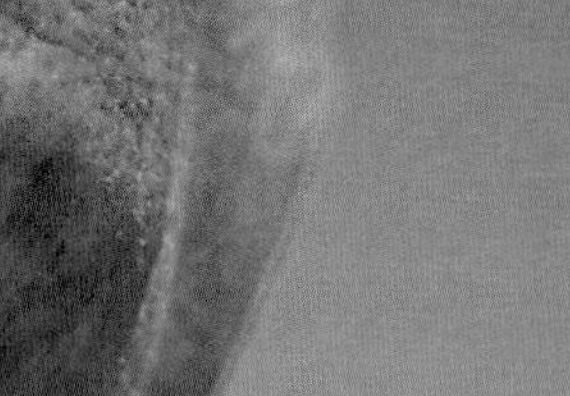

**2**

**3**

**4**

**5**

**6**

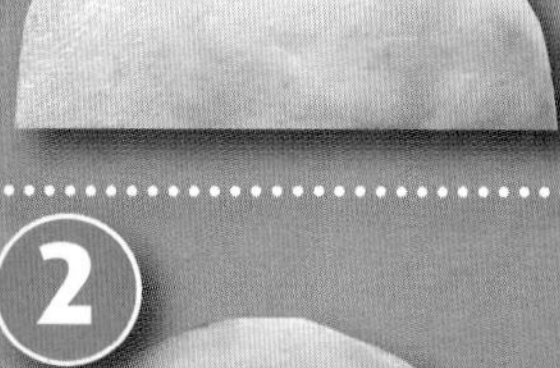

**A** Raul Meireles

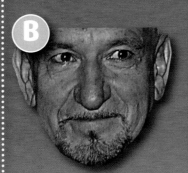

**B** Ben Kingsley

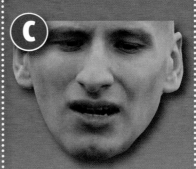

**C** Jonjo Shelvey

**D** Jordan

**E** Paul Konchesky

**F** Ross Kemp

**G** Jay Spearing

**H** Kojak

**I** Joe Cole

**J** Gail Porter

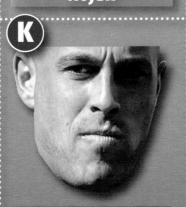

**K** Pepe Reina

**L** Jimmy Hill

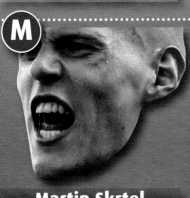

**M** Martin Skrtel

**N** Boy George

**O** Reina/Konchesky

**7**

**8**

**9**

**10**

**11**

**12**

**13**

**14**

**15**

13

# THE MEN KENNY REJECTED

**Picture exclusive revealing the men who didn't make Kenny's shortlist to become our new manager**

Jeff Stelling as your number two and Charlie Nicholas and Alan McInally on your coaching staff? Nah, forget it Thommo

Sorry Digger, you've been unsuccessful. But have you got a number for Les Parry?

Sorry Skippy, not sure another Aussie with a ponytail would go down well on the Kop

What d'ya think about bringing Graeme Souness back?

Fancy disagreeing with more American owners Martin lad?

If I promise to not play eight full-backs a game again will you give **me** the job?

Meanwhile, there were rumours that Inter Milan had a highly rated manager who Kenny thought might be interested in the job...

Any chance, Rafa?

## Next time:

**How Sven's interview went & why Jurgen Klinsmann turned down the job**

Back   Forward   Stop   Refresh   Home   AutoFill   Print   Mail

 **Anything and everything a Kopite exclusively made-up website and you've always promised yourself.**

| All Items | Auctions | Buy It Now |

football magazine        Sporting Goods

☐ Search title **and** description

**COCKNEY DICTIONARY**   Bids: **23**   Time remaining: **3hrs 33mins**

A guide to learning the lingo of full backs, managers and promising midfielders from the south

Bald left-backs who struggle to live up to Julian Dicks' standard and a midfield prodigy who doesn't play much are known to speak it

**BODY WARMER**   Bids: **2**   Time remaining: **-30 years**

Questionable fashion accessory worn by new boy and leading star alike to keep warm during UK summers

They've been seen at Melwood more than in the Back to the Future Trilogy where a 'feel-good factor' was replaced by 'look-bad factor'

**IMODIUM**   Bids: **0**   Time remaining: **EXPIRED**

Tablet used to combat diarrhoea so you can still be available for that all important match. Suitable for injury-prone Italians

Failure to take will result in missing games for pathetic reasons throughout a season, if indeed reasons were actually genuine anyway

**BOARDROOM CHAIR**   Bids: **5**   Time remaining: **2years**

Executive chair not used for almost a year. Boardroom pending refurbishment believed to apparently knock your sox off

Perfect for sitting at your desk and sending abusive and unprofessional emails to genuine fans frustrated at the decline of a once great football club

**TAXIS**   Bids: **500,000**   Time remaining: **Until summer**

Form of transport to take you from one place to another, regardless of how long you've been there

Perfect for getting rid of immobile Danes, Fulham-standard full-backs and twittering wingers, sorry, strikers...

**UMBRELLA**   Bids: **1**   Time remaining: **Until new ownership**

For those who are in an already ridiculously humiliating situation and don't mind looking like Steve McClaren

Proven to keep you dry in downpours when watching your side play out one of its worst results in history despite you being out of your depth

Internet zone

wants can be found on Lfcbay. Just log on to our bid for that super hero costume or body warmer Here's just a few of the items that are on sale . . .

click here)

| ▲▼ | **Search** | Refine Search |

## CALENDAR Bids: 1    Time remaining: **2months 4days**

Calendar complete with football fixtures to remind ginger Scottish manager that season starts in August

Those who continually save their good work until it is far too late may have use in learning when the football season runs from

## LFC SEASON REVIEW 09/10    Bids: 2    Time remaining: **12months**

An easy way to get information out of a Red by subjecting him to three hours of torture

Unless your name is Alex Ferguson or Rat Boy then you are unlikely to enjoy this overpriced DVD

## WORLD CRUISE    Bids: 1    Time remaining: **EXPIRED**

A perfect way to escape the trials of a difficult year at work and to get away while your mates play at the World Cup

Tickets booked in advance before change of plans saw seller return to previous role on temporary basis

## CAPTAIN'S ARMBAND    Bids: 5    Time remaining: **10months**

Worn by legendary club figures now tainted by multiple bearers

Value reduced after five owners in space of two months, from European Cup-winning captains to back-up defenders deployed as strikers against a League Two side

## MELWOOD'S NO.20 LOCKER    Bids: 1    Time remaining: **4Ever**

Spacious storage locker in between others owned by a lazy rapper and sideways-thinking Brazilian

Reputation tainted twice now by locker owners known as traitors by one club or another. You would be barm(b)y to miss out on this deal

## TOM HICKS IN HIS COAT    Bids: **Loads**    Time remaining: **Erm...**

Not only a clothing item that keeps you warm and dry, but also a signal that you are leaving somewhere

Regardless of whether it means one American consortium replaces another, there are sure to be plenty of bids for this so get in early

# SPIRIT OF DOCHERTY

## THE NEWTON HEATH SUPPORTERS UNION

# S.O.D's LAW

- To represent the best interests of the supporters of Newton Heath

- To force the Glazers out by wearing green and gold scarves because that will really do the job

- To improve the standard and value of long-haul flights to home games

- To make up more songs about Scousers because we don't have enough

- To ensure that banner about City not winning anything since 1976 gets updated

- To remind the club to turn up the volume on the PA System before kick-off as soon as away fans start singing

- To get behind the Red Knights in their quest to own Newton Heath FC

- To go and support FC United of Bury instead when the Red Knights bugger off

George Gillett and Tom Hicks finally put the club up for sale in April, while Rafa Benitez was left with the problem of Alberto Aquilani on his hands

we've got the
BEST MIDFIELD
IN THE...

**XABI ALONSO**

One footballer put his Teletubbies house up for sale in July, and it was your job to guess who...

THE KOP ANNUAL

# WHO WOULD LIVE IN A HOUSE LIKE THIS?

THROUGH THE KEYHOLE

### Clue 1

To the front of the property is large grassed area, about the size of a soccer pitch, with a large balcony area on the second floor that is perfect for sitting on and watching football, something the current owner has spent most of his time doing in recent years.

### Clue 2

One of the grandest rooms in the property, the dining hall is perfect for the most sumptuous of banquets and has adequate space for 14 guests to be entertained, although this remains a theoretical number as the vendor doesn't have that many friends. Anybody wishing to serve pans of Scouse in this room need not apply.

### Clue 3

With the property arranged into four floors, this sweeping circular staircase has provided ideal access for the gentleman of the house who thinks nothing of making sweeping statements that will never be forgotten. It could be said that the staircase is a something of a rat-run for the rest of the house.

### Clue 4

Comfort is of the essence for the elderly owner and the neutrally coloured lounge provides him a relaxing ambience for boiling up with rage in front of the television when his least favourite football team scores a goal. He has also spent many a happy hour say here trying to grow a proper moustache.

### Clue 5

Designed to a high specification, the kitchen area has oodles of space for preparing prawn sandwiches, storing bottles of bitter and drawing up plans for an eco-friendly carbon-neutral Teletubbies style house that pisses your neighbours off so much they complain and planning permission gets refused.

### Clue 6

Complete with a specially made pool table for dwarves, the games room towards the rear of the property may not have any other games in it, but it does have some spectacular views. The owner has ensured nothing can detract from them by avoiding installing any mirrors, or pictures of his brother, throughout the entire house.

### Clue 7

One of six exquisite bathrooms. May seem excessive, but the present owner is full of s**t. The throne in the corner is ideal for sitting on while spurting verbal diarrhoea and the large bath comes recommended by the owner's Serbian friend who spends a lot of time in one while football matches he was taking part in are continuing.

### Clue 8

No country estate manor house would be complete without the obligatory home cinema, a fitting venue to not watch Brookside, Bread, Boys from the Blackstuff or LFC TV.

**with (Larry) Loyd Grossman**

So there you have it. The rat-run feature staircase. No mirrors on the walls. The Kop under the pool. Who would live in a house like this? Kopites, it's over to you...

### And Finally...

And finally foot piece de resistance, the room of the mansion that has added a good £5.5 million to its £6 million asking price. The leisure suite comes complete with gym, Jacuzzi and swimming pool but it is what is underneath the pool that makes this house so special. To mark the owner's love of the beautiful game, a copy of The Kop Magazine and a Liverpool Football Club scarf have been buried beneath it – something he must think about every time he goes for a swim.

# Finger lickin', LFC nickin' takeaway

THE chips might have been down for Liverpool FC but that hasn't stopped this cheeky takeaway from naming their shop after the club. We've all been for a KFC – Wayne Rooney is better with a box meal than a penalty box these days – and now you can go for an LFC on Lord Street. You'll never eat alone at Liverpool Fried Chicken according to their sign, which is another clever play on words as Liverpool Football Club's motto has recently been 'you'll never pay a loan'.

■ After Nabil El Zhar joined PAOK on a season long loan, we received a call in the office from a Greek radio station asking for someone to go on air and tell supporters of the club what they can expect from their new winger. We politely declined...

# THE KOP MOLE

*With all the EXCLUSIVE news from 2010*

## BLUES TOP? FAT CHANCE

■ AN online survey by NHS Choices says Everton have some of the least healthy fans in the country.

Not only do many of them talk rubbish, they apparently eat a lot of it too with over 50% of the Bluenoses surveyed being at an unhealthy weight. That's what happens when you've got Yakubu as a role model.

Sunderland have the most unhealthy fans of all – many are fatter than Steve Bruce's head – while us Liverpool supporters are the 6th fittest bunch, possibly because no-one can afford a half-time pie any more with the ticket prices going up.

However, I have to take issue with the survey for suggesting that Newcastle fans are supposedly the fifth fittest in the country. What about Mike Ashley? He not only looks like everything he wears begins in two XX's, but is also paying the price for his massive BMI – Big Mistake Investing.

| | Team | % of fans who are an unhealthy weight |
|---|---|---|
| 1 | Sunderland | 51.3 |
| 2 | Everton | 51.16 |
| 3 | Wigan Athletic | 48.21 |
| 4 | Manchester City | 47.25 |
| 5 | Fulham | 47.17 |
| 6 | Blackburn Rovers | 45.0 |
| 7 | West Ham United | 44.99 |
| 8 | Bolton Wanderers | 44.9 |
| 9 | Wolverhampton Wanderers | 44.89 |
| 10 | Tottenham Hotspur | 44.87 |
| 11 | West Bromwich Albion | 44.63 |
| 12 | Aston Villa | 43.23 |
| 13 | Stoke City | 42.19 |
| 14 | Birmingham City | 41.49 |
| 15 | Liverpool | 40.5 |
| 16 | Newcastle United | 40.32 |
| 17 | Chavski | 38.48 |
| 18 | Newton Heath | 36.39 |
| 19 | Arsenal | 36.3 |
| 20 | Blackpool | 30.33 |

# Torres is a hero

THIS was the year Fernando Torres was turned into comic book hero called 'Super Deportistas' in Spain with the Liverpool number nine fighting gladiators and lions using his brute strength and, er, a ball.

## TYPICAL GERMANS!

Now digging out even more Kop goss and dishing even more dirt on our rivals!

*Follow us at twitter.com/thekopmagazine*

## Milan ponders pigeon holes

MILAN Jovanovic made quite an impression down at Melwood as he settled into life as a Liverpool player. The Serbian international has been finding his way around the Reds training base and, being a friendly chap, stops to talk to visitors in reception. On one occasion he even whipped out half a bar of chocolate he'd brought back from Liverpool's Swiss training camp from his Louis Vitton bag and offered it to a journalist who was waiting so speak to Joe Cole!

But Jovanovic hasn't completely adjusted to life in England yet and there were rather amusing scenes when the Melwood receptionist tried to explain to him how the concept of the pigeonhole system for the players' personal mail works. I'm told that the confused looking Serb could be heard muttering 'pigeon? pigeon?' to himself as he wandered around Melwood for a couple of minutes.

## SIGHTS FOR SORE EYES

STILL shocked at seeing Michael Owen in a Liverpool shirt at Carra's testimonial? Never thought you'd see the day when one of them wore a Liver Bird upon his chest in front of the Kop at Anfield?

You can't have been at Big Ron Yeats' testimonial against Celtic at Anfield in May 1974, then, when Newton Heath's greatest player of all time pulled on a Liverpool shirt.

Celtic were the visitors for Rowdy's benefit match and appearing as a guest for them that night was Sir Bobby Charlton, who had retired from playing 12 months earlier but was using the match for a run-out ahead of his comeback as player-manager of Preston North End.

Before kick-off, the teams came out on to the pitch wearing each others shirts and Charlton, complete with comb-over flapping in the wind, posed for a picture with Yeats in front of the Kop.

He enjoyed it so much that he brought a Bobby Charlton XI to Anfield three years later for Tommy Smith's testimonial and wore a Liverpool kit again!

So here is Bobby Charlton pictured in the most famous red football shirt he ever wore.

The second most famous was England's.

**While we won't blame Everton if they only wear their pink number the once, we certainly won't let them forget about it...**

# HERE IS HOW TO WEAR PINK

**...AND HERE'S HOW NOT TO**

**Even so, they're right. The fuchsia's bright...**

'Rafa signings' Milan Jovanovic and Danny Wilson enrolled at their new school ahead of their new term in August, along with Bosman buy of the summer Joe Cole, who would soon serve a three-match detention

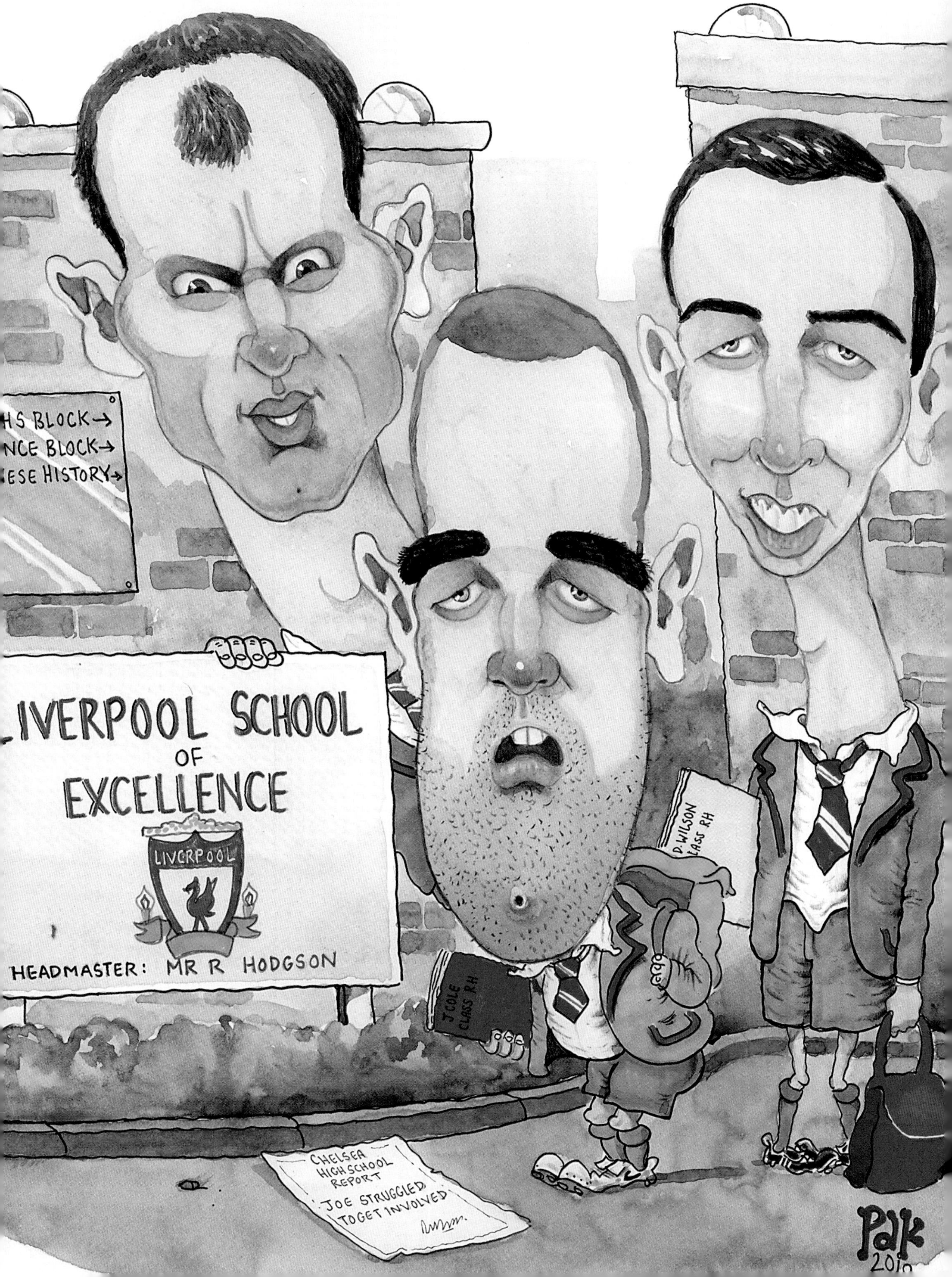

THE KOP CARTOON

HS BLOCK →
NCE BLOCK →
ESE HISTORY →

LIVERPOOL SCHOOL OF EXCELLENCE

LIVERPOOL

HEADMASTER: MR R HODGSON

J COLE CLASS RH

D.WILSON CLASS RH

CHELSEA HIGH SCHOOL REPORT
'JOE STRUGGLED TO GET INVOLVED'

PAK 2010

# The best of SPOTTED

**Margi Clarke** in the Everyman Bistro clutching a Primark Bag.

**Henry Winkler** – aka the Fonz – at Lime Street station.

Henry 'The Fonz' Winkler at a match pretending to know about football

Starsailor's **James Walsh** and The Rascals' **Greg Mighall** and **Joe Edwards** on location on Parr Street, during filming of the movie version of Kevin Sampson's 'Powder'.

**Neil Mellor** shopping in the sales in Marks & Spencer, Ormskirk.

**Dani Pacheco** walking through arrivals at John Lennon International Airport in the early hours of January 5 – a few hours before it was shut due to the snow.

**David Fairclough** chatting to a rather rotund, balding postman on a train into Liverpool.

**Sotirios**

**Kyrgiakos** looking annoyed that there wasn't any bread left in Tesco, Old Hall Street, on the day the Spurs match should've been played on.

**Kerry Fowler**, wife of God, with a pram outside Mango, Liverpool One.

**Gerard Houllier** in the club shop at Anfield on the day the Spurs game should've been played.

Frankie Goes to Hollywood's Liverpool-supporting guitarist 'Nasher', aka **Brian Nash**, watching Sex & Drugs & Rock & Roll (the Ian Drury biopic) at FACT, Wood Street.

**Alex Curran**, checking her hair in the visor mirror of her white Range Rover as she drove down the Formby bypass.

**Neil Fitzmaurice** having a bevy in the Sir Thomas Hotel the night after the Reading defeat.

**Sotirios Kyrgiakos** buying bananas in Tesco, Old Hall Street, the day after he scored at Stoke.

Free drinks for Stevie?: Lily Allen's announcement that he was in the MEN crowd was met by boos...

Liverpool 1-Odeon: Dirk and family like the pictures

Newcastle owner **Mike Ashley** dancing (badly) in the Apt bar on Queens Street, London, the night after Liverpool v Spurs.

**Alex McLeish** drinking scotch in the bar of the Hilton Hotel, Liverpool City Centre, the night before Birmingham dumped Everton out of the FA Cup.

**Pepe Reina** with his family at the Odeon, Liverpool One, on FA Cup fourth-round Saturday.

**Sotirios Kyrgiakos** leaving the dry cleaners on Old Hall Street the day before the Bolton match in January.

**John Barnes** with family walking past David M Robinson jewellers, Liverpool One, a couple of days after the Bolton game.

**Daniel Ayala** and **Dani Pacheco** having a meal in La Vina, North John Street, a couple of nights before the February's Merseyside derby.

Former Everton chief executive **Keith Wyness** tucking into a large baguette at Euston Station.

**Kenny Dalglish, Steven Gerrard, Jamie Carragher, Sammy Lee, Jay Spearing, Dani Pacheco** and **Paul Ince** all at Anfield for Liverpool Under-18s' FA Youth Cup defeat to Watford.

**Dirk Kuyt** with his family at the Odeon, Liverpool One, on the Saturday before the Unirea home game.

Scouse gymnast **Beth Tweddle** at the Vue Cinema, Cheshire Oaks.

**Alan Green** screaming down his microphone that he hadn't passed the Man City v Liverpool team news on earlier because he didn't have it earlier inside Eastlands.

Former Reds chief executive **Rick Parry** sat behind the Liverpool bench at the same game in February.

The OC star **Tate Donovan** with his kids in the children's play area, Bleecker Street in Greenwich Village, New York.

**Stig Inge Bjornebye** and his wife stood outside Top Man, Liverpool One, a couple of days after the City game.

**John Barnes** holding hands with a blonde female companion as they walked past the

Hard Day's Night Hotel, North John Street, the day before Unirea away.

Reds supporting comedian **John Bishop** stood outside John Lewis in Liverpool One.

**Abigail Clancy** going down the escalator to the car park in Liverpool One a few days after February's Blackburn game.

**Natasha Hamilton** shopping in Espirit on the same afternoon.

**Sammy Lee** walking around Melwood singing Van Morrison's Brown Eyed Girl very loudly during the spring international midweek.

**Steven Gerrard** getting booed at the MEN after **Lily Allen** announced live on stage that he was in the crowd watching her and **Dizzee Rascal**.

**Drew Schofield**, star of 15 Minutes That Shook The World, in the Hen & Chickens, Melling, the night before Lille away.

Former Blues winger **Kevin Sheedy** stood inside Moorfields station looking rather puzzled.

**Maxi Rodriguez** pushing a pram past the Everton shop in Liverpool One on the day of the Lille home match.

Ex-Everton defender **John Bailey** stood outside La Vina, reading the menu while clutching four cans of Fosters.

**Jay Spearing** in the Mersey Clipper pub next to Prenton Park before Tranmere v Hartlepool.

A scruffy looking **Jimmy Case** near Victoria Station, London, during the week after the Newton Heath game in March.

**Kenny Dalglish** at Southport tip dumping rubbish three hours before attending the 3-0 win over Sunderland.

**Ronnie Moran** at Melwood a few days before Benfica away.

**Neil Fitzmaurice**

trying to engage in some banter with a stag do at Aintree racecourse on the Thursday of the Grand National meeting.

**Ian Snodin** putting bets on in William Hill, Old Hall Street, on the afternoon of Benfica's trip to Anfield.

**Jimmy Case** in Smokie Mo's, Brownlow Hill, after the Grand National.

DIY SOS presenter **Nick Knowles** chatting with Kopites in the Emirates Lounge at Dubai airport the day before volcanic ash grounded all flights.

**Sir Bobby Charlton** at the Albert Dock a couple of hours before attending the Hillsborough memorial service at Anfield.

**Steven Gerrard** getting out of a Ford Focus and using the cash machine at the BP

**Hop to it: Beth Tweddle off to the cinema**

**John Bishop**

Garage in Freshfield.

Radio City's **Pete Price** pushing past a woman in Lime Street Station.

Saints RLFC full-back **Paul Wellens** having a pint in the Java Bar, St Helens after their Challenge Cup win over Toulouse.

**Willy Russell** doing his weekly shop wearing a suit in Tesco, Woolton.

**Philipp Degen** in Tesco, Mather Avenue, the day before the 3-0 victory against West Ham in April.

**Jordy Brouwer** in Starbucks, Liverpool One, on the afternoon of the West Ham game.

**Ray Clemence** chatting to **John Aldridge** inside Anfield later that night when Aldo should have been on air with Radio City!

**Daniel Ayala** with a leggy blonde at the back of the queue inside 2 Joes Milkshakes, Liverpool One.

**Jason McAteer** driving his Range Rover through Ince Woods.

**Soto's shopping list: No bread left in Tesco**

# 1953/54 revisited

The start of the 2010/11 season saw the Reds playing poorly, losing to the likes of Northampton and Blackpool, plummeting into the relegation zone and reviving memories of the catastrophic 1953/54 season when the Reds last dropped out of the top flight. It left some fans wondering if the worst could happen again...

**Back row (left to right):** Monty Skrtel, Percy Reina, Ronnie Meireles
**Middle row:** Dick Kuyt, Lenny Leiva, Dougie Agger, Stan Kyrgiakos, Charlie Poulsen, Joe Cole and Donald Ngog
**Front row:** Matty Rodriguez, Frankie Torres, Cedrick Gerrard, Jack Carragher, Alf Johnson

# THE KOP MOLE'S PAPARAZZI PICS

When it comes to getting those highly sought after snaps, the Kop Mole is always one step ahead of the game. Over the last 12 months football's most famous gossip columnist has given Kop Magazine readers exclusive after exclusive. He talks us through some of his best pics of 2010

VISITORS to Liverpool's Academy have been left doing double-takes after apparently being greeted by Fabio Capello at the entrance to the Under-18s' training complex.

And only when 'Fabio' emerges from the gate-house and speaks do they realise that it isn't actually the Italian bloke who thinks Stevie G is a left-winger and Emile Heskey a goalscoring striker that is stood before them.

Head of security Jay Fitzpatrick is a dead-ringer for the England manager and with so many people commenting on him being a Capello look-a-like during the World Cup, Academy manager John Owens decided it was about time he dressed like the Italian.

"I used to work for the FA taking their England 'C' team," John told me, "choosing players from Conference level downwards to play the likes of Holland and Italy. Jay is a real look-a-like for Fabio so I fitted him out with my old blazer and tie to help him to look the part!"

He should give the FA a ring – they might offer him a £6 million deal to stand outside Soho Square...

TEN years ago French World Cup winner Bernard Diomede signed for Liverpool, but such was his lack of impact at Anfield that his Reds career is best forgotten.

However, the move did work out well for someone – Bernard's brother Willy.

Having been captivated by Liverpool's culture and met his wife Dee in the city, Willy Diomede is still living here now and works as a chef in the swanky Racquet Club's 'Ziba' restaurant on Chapel Street.

Pictured is one of Diomede's signature dishes – scallops with beetroot and orange risotto.

Well, he is called Willy...

CONGRATULATIONS to Sophie Fairclough, daughter of Liverpool hero David, who won the Aintree Style 2010 competition at the Grand National.

Amongst the prizes that Formby-based Sophie won were a new car and 10-day holiday to Barbados and all because she looked stunning in her silk emerald green dress.

Isn't it amazing what her dad can do with a couple of St Etienne shirts and a needle?

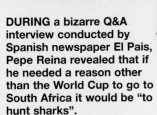

DURING a bizarre Q&A interview conducted by Spanish newspaper El Pais, Pepe Reina revealed that if he needed a reason other than the World Cup to go to South Africa it would be "to hunt sharks".

Perhaps it was a good thing that he spent the whole of the tournament on the bench as FIFA wouldn't have needed goal-line technology to spot one of them in his net.

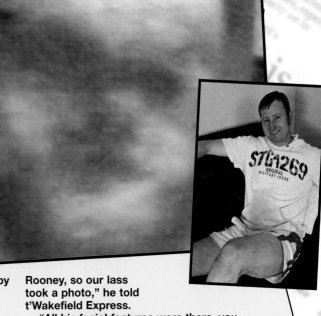

AFTER Newton Heath supporter Rich Rigby of Wakefield fell off his off-road bike he suffered a knee injury, but what he didn't expect was Wayne Rooney's face to appear on it.

Despite the injury, he hobbled to the alehouse to show his knee to his mates and it was then that Rooney's unmistakable Shrek-like features became apparent. "I were havin' drink wit friends and when I showed 'em knee we realised it looked like Rooney, so our lass took a photo," he told t'Wakefield Express.

"All his facial features were there, you could see his small ears, nose and he even had a beard like the real Rooney."

Fortunately for pensioners in Yorkshire the swelling went down and Rich's Roo-knee (see what I've done there?) disappeared before it got near them.

Now that's what you call a freak injury...

# THE KOP MOLE'S PAPARAZZI PICS

OUT of all their former players, Paddy Crerand is generally recognised as the most die-hard, steadfast, obsessive, biased, bitter and somewhat twisted Newton Heath supporter.

He's also said to hate Scousers, but this photo, taken behind the scenes at MUTV, suggests that the grizzly Glaswegian may actually be a closet Kopite.

Why else would he be giving a five-fingered salute?

SOME pictures speak louder than words...

THE weather had been so bad that it isn't just Didier Drogba who has had trouble staying on his feet.

With so much ice on the ground not even football club chairmen have been safe from the big freeze.

Tranmere Rovers chairman Peter Johnson was spotted walking through Oxton Village until he slipped on an icy patch and crashed to the ground, landing on his arse.

I'm told that 'Red Johnno' went down quicker than it looked like Everton would when he owned them.

Meanwhile, Kopite Stephen Haw from St Helens made the most of the big freeze by making a snowman-ager and sending a picture of it to liverpoolfc.tv.

It's a good likeness, although the snow version does seem a little more animated than Rafa used to get when Liverpool scored.

CONGRATULATIONS to Daniel Agger who married finacee Sophie Nelson in his home town of Hvidovre on May 15.

Judging by his suit, the Dane either went to the same tailor as our 1996 FA Cup final team, or he's a big James Bond fan. Wonder if he'll change his squad number to 007?

IF you're getting married this year then I hope you've got the must-have fashion accessory.

Well, your wedding day won't be complete unless you walk down the aisle wearing a big white scarf – just like Joseph Yobo did.

The Everton defender tied the knot with girl-friend Adaeze Igwe in a midnight "crossover" service in Nigeria.

Yobo only met his new wife in 2009, and according to the couple it was "love at first sight", which was lucky as Ada was seven months pregnant at the wedding.

The Blues' centre-half has denied the pregnancy had anything to do with how quick they got married, saying: "To show how serious my intentions were, I even met with her family to assure them that she was in safe hands.

"Her mom immediately approved the relationship so we took it further from that moment onwards." Brings a whole new meaning to being away on international duty, eh?

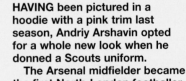

HAVING been pictured in a hoodie with a pink trim last season, Andriy Arshavin opted for a whole new look when he donned a Scouts uniform.

The Arsenal midfielder became the first North-London footballer to associate himself with the Scout Movement since Spurs signed Chris Woggle to promote a junior Gunners event that saw 200 young Arsenal fans camp out on the pitch at The Emirates.

Unsurprisingly, they weren't allowed to light a campfire by the club but it wasn't a problem as there'd have been no singing around it anyway due to them being Arsenal supporters.

# KOP CLASSIFIEDS

## Consultants

**INTERESTED** in buying a football club and need some advice? Call R Parry on 0101 53LL 0UT for how not to do it

## Dancing

**TAKE** up line dancing lessons with LL&CP productions. We specialise in side to side routines. Call 0151 21 28 and don't pass (or shoot, or tackle) up the opportunity.

## Moving home

**LOOKING** to not learn English? Fed up living in a country where they don't speak Spanish and you're sick of the weather? Call 'Mrs M', Barcelona for advice on how to issue your other half with an ultimatum to get your own way.

## Bank loans

## For Sale

**BRAND** new, much talked about, previously unused spade. £600m. Never before put in the ground. One previous owner. Comes with 60 day guarantee or your club back. NB: any guarantees are a lie.

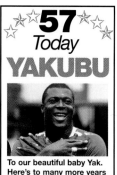

**57 Today YAKUBU**

To our beautiful baby Yak. Here's to many more years of ~~greatness~~ mediocrity. Love and best wishes, EFC x

## HOLIDAYS

VISIT CROSBY

**Looking for somewhere different this summer? Do you love art, football and culture? Then come to Crosby, home of the famous Anfield Iron Men statues, Antony Gormley's permanent tribute to Liverpool legend Tommy Smith. One stroll along the beach and you'll be ready to start a riot in a graveyard, or at least develop a hatred of crazy horses. Book now and get a kick in the shins on arrival absolutely free!**

## Health

**OUT** of work? Your contract not being renewed due to your unreliable fitness? Then get in touch with a Fab specialist health firm that will blag your way to a new deal so you are financially secure. Play football with your kids safe in the knowledge that work will understand. Contact Aureli-ows now on 0151 ACHILLES. Our 100th customer will receive a free Brazilian, but not an Arshavin as they are too expensive.

## Wanted

**GOALKEEPER** must have two hands. Ability to catch a ball not necessary. Call Arsene before January.

## Wanted

**RED SOX** needed for football club with red socks but no dosh. All donations gratefully received, contact M Broughton.

## BEAUTY

### Surgery Gone Wrong?

**BEFORE**          **AFTER**

**Plastic Surgeons You Can Trust. Discreet service. Former clients include Jimmy Bullard, Carlos Tevez and Gareth Bale. Speak in confidence to Gary on 0161 0161.**

## PUBLIC SPEAKING

**HAVING** a homecoming party? Want to be the centre of attention? Then come to Jose's Manuel classes – Jose **P**res**E**nts public s**P**eaking l**E**cture**S**. **PEPE'S** – sign up today! Held every two years.

## Books

**ALBERTO'S** Book of Sickie Excuses will teach you how to shy off work any day of the week – especially those annoying outdoor weekend shifts. Includes a 12 month money-back guarantee if you perform well in your next job.

**LEE MASON'S** brand new release (notebook size) is packed full of stats on Liverpool players and their work-related mishaps. Part One of an infinite series. Coming soon, Stuart Attwell's new classic collection: 'The goals I didn't see'.

**THE KOP ANNUAL 2011** One previously used copy, currently being read on the classifieds page. Will end up on ebay if owner can be arsed scanning in front cover and uploading it.

Tom Hicks Junior made the headlines in January when his email gaffe ironically blew up in his face as he lost his place on the board. And he wasn't too old to be put over his daddy's knee because of it...

THE KOP CARTOON

THE REDS OF LIVERPOOL

GO US DODGERS!

KEEPING YOUR COOL

Ryan Babel 19 tweeter
GOTBALL .. LOST IT .....
AND AGAIN.....
YOU HAVE EMAIL
NO PARENTAL CONTROL
SOS    FACEBOOK

BLOW FOOTBALL

THE DAILY TRIPE
SACK THE MANAGER!
BY SEVERAL EX-PLAYERS WHO FAILED MISERABLY AS MANAGERS

2010

## Geordie State of Mind (part II) (with apologies to Alicia Keys)

Oooohh, New Castle
Oooohh, New Castle

Grew up in a toon,
That is famous as a place
of rubbish teams,
Gazza's always loud
Alan Shearer took 'em down
And the blokes ain't lean,
If I can't get laid here
I can't get laid anywhere
That's what they say,
Carroll gets in fights
On Bigg Market party nights
down toon, haway

Even if we ain't got great teams
I got my deluded dreams

Haway I'm from New Castle
Geordie jungle where dreams are made up
There's nothing you can win
Now you're in New Castle

These shirts we all look the same too
Like zebras from the zoo
Hear it for New Castle, New Castle,
New Castle

On the Gallowgate
There ain't nowt to celebrate
Ladies caked in lard

Ashley spent a lot
Kevin Keegan lost the plot
Geordies call him God

Hail a Geordie cab
Takes me down from Byker
To the old Tyne Bridge

Lads in black and white
with a hunger for
More than in Gazza's fridge

Gonna blow it by any means
I got my deluded dreams

Haway I'm from New Castle
Geordie jungle where dreams are made up
There's nothing you can win
Now you're in New Castle

These shirts we all look the same too
Like zebras from the zoo
Hear it for New Castle, New Castle,
New Castle

One shoe in the air for Ameobi
He's shite, but makes Barton look pretty
No place in the world that can compare
Put yer shoes up in the air
Everybody say yeah, yeah, yeah, yeah

New Castle
Geordie jungle where dreams are made up
There's nothing you can win
Now you're in New Castle

These shirts we all look the same too
Like zebras from the zoo
Hear it for New Castle!

**THE KOP Karaoke**

Kopites like nothing more than a good sing-song. Here's a few alternative tunes you might hear getting belted out at The Kop Christmas knees-up this year

## Hot N Cold (with apologies to Katy Perry)

You change our minds
Like a girl changes clothes
Yeah you tweet your mates
Like you've just bought a phone

And you overplay
So we speak critically
We should know
That you're no go for L-FC

Cause you're hot then you're cold
You're grim then you're gold
You're in then you're out
You're Cole then you're Kuyt

You're dull then you're bright
You're great then you're shite
You shoot, we stand up
You pass, you fuck up

You! You don't really want to stay, no?
You! But you don't really want to go-o

You're hot then you're cold
You quick then you're slow
You're in then you're out
You're Cole then you're Kuyt

(instrumental)

You could so be

On our wing, so in sync
But your attitude
At times, it does stink

How we loved, your scoring
Then you're plain boring
We should know
That you're not gonna change

Cause you're hot then you're cold
Want you kept want you sold
You're in, then you're out
What's the rapping about?

You play like a star
You drive a flash car
You lay down a track
We get on your back

You! You don't really want to play, no?
You! But you don't really wanna go, Rio?

You're hot then you're cold
You hide then you're bold
You're in then you're out
You're Cole then you're Kuyt

(instrumental)

Someone tell the rabble
Got a case of a Ryan Babel
Stuck on a rollercoaster

Can't get in our side

You change our minds
Like a girl changes clothes

Cause you're hot then you're cold
You're grim then you're gold
You're in then you're out
You're Cole then you're Kuyt

You're dull then you're bright
You're great then you're shite
You shoot, we stand up
You pass, you fuck up

Cause you're hot then you're cold
Want you kept want you sold
You're in, then you're out
What's the rapping about?

You play like a star
You drive a flash car
You lay down a track
We get on your back

You! You don't really want to stay, no?
You! But you don't really want to go-o

You're hot then you're cold
You're quick then you're slow
You're in then you're out
You're Cole then you're Kuyt...

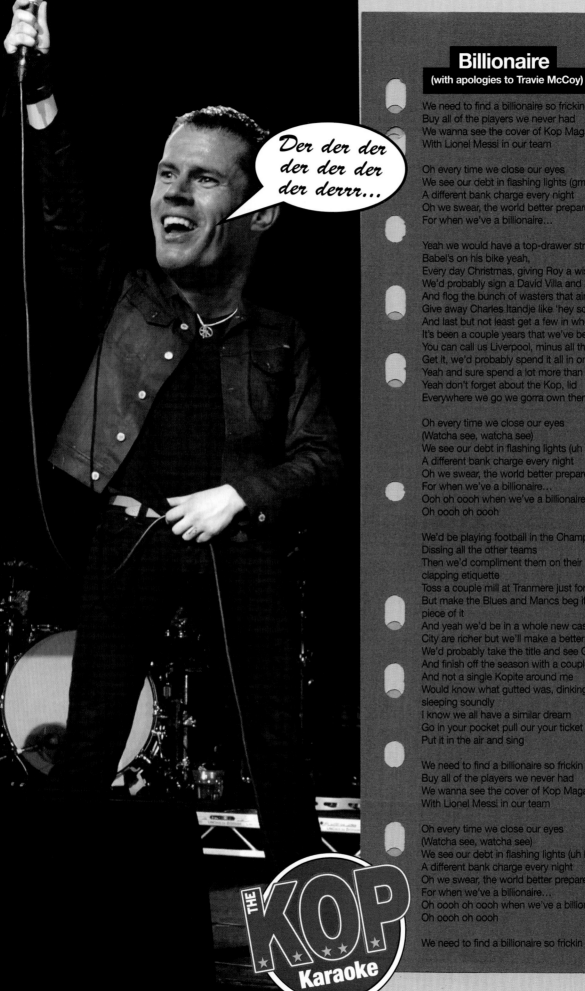

## Billionaire
**(with apologies to Travie McCoy)**

We need to find a billionaire so frickin bad
Buy all of the players we never had
We wanna see the cover of Kop Magazine
With Lionel Messi in our team

Oh every time we close our eyes
We see our debt in flashing lights (grrr)
A different bank charge every night
Oh we swear, the world better prepare
For when we've a billionaire…

Yeah we would have a top-drawer striker
Babel's on his bike yeah,
Every day Christmas, giving Roy a wish list
We'd probably sign a David Villa and a top Brit
And flog the bunch of wasters that aint never done shit
Give away Charles Itandje like 'hey someone have this'
And last but not least get a few in who are English
It's been a couple years that we've been skint so
You can call us Liverpool, minus all the dough though
Get it, we'd probably spend it all in one hit
Yeah and sure spend a lot more than the Yanks did
Yeah don't forget about the Kop, lid
Everywhere we go we gorra own theme music

Oh every time we close our eyes
(Watcha see, watcha see)
We see our debt in flashing lights (uh huh uh huh)
A different bank charge every night
Oh we swear, the world better prepare
For when we've a billionaire…
Ooh oh oooh when we've a billionaire
Oh oooh oh oooh

We'd be playing football in the Champions League
Dissing all the other teams
Then we'd compliment them on their post-match
clapping etiquette
Toss a couple mill at Tranmere just for the heck of it
But make the Blues and Mancs beg if they want a
piece of it
And yeah we'd be in a whole new cash bracket
City are richer but we'll make a better crack of it
We'd probably take the title and see Gerrard lift it up
And finish off the season with a couple more silver cups
And not a single Kopite around me
Would know what gutted was, dinking well,
sleeping soundly
I know we all have a similar dream
Go in your pocket pull our your ticket
Put it in the air and sing

We need to find a billionaire so frickin bad
Buy all of the players we never had
We wanna see the cover of Kop Magazine
With Lionel Messi in our team

Oh every time we close our eyes
(Watcha see, watcha see)
We see our debt in flashing lights (uh huh uh huh)
A different bank charge every night
Oh we swear, the world better prepare
For when we've a billionaire…
Oh oooh oh oooh when we've a billionaire
Oh oooh oh oooh

We need to find a billionaire so frickin bad…

# THE BIG POWER STRUGGLE 2010

# LEADERS' DEBATE
## POLL RESULTS JUST IN!

# THE NEW MANAGER VOTE 2010

Hughes: Got 0 % of the vote

Alex McLeish: Got the same as Sparky

Steve Bruce: No big 'eads at Anfield

Peter Snow even got out his Anfield swingometer as we searched for someone to replace Rafa

we've got the
**BEST MIDFIELD**
**IN THE...**

# Cashley's last throw of the dice to get Cheryl back...

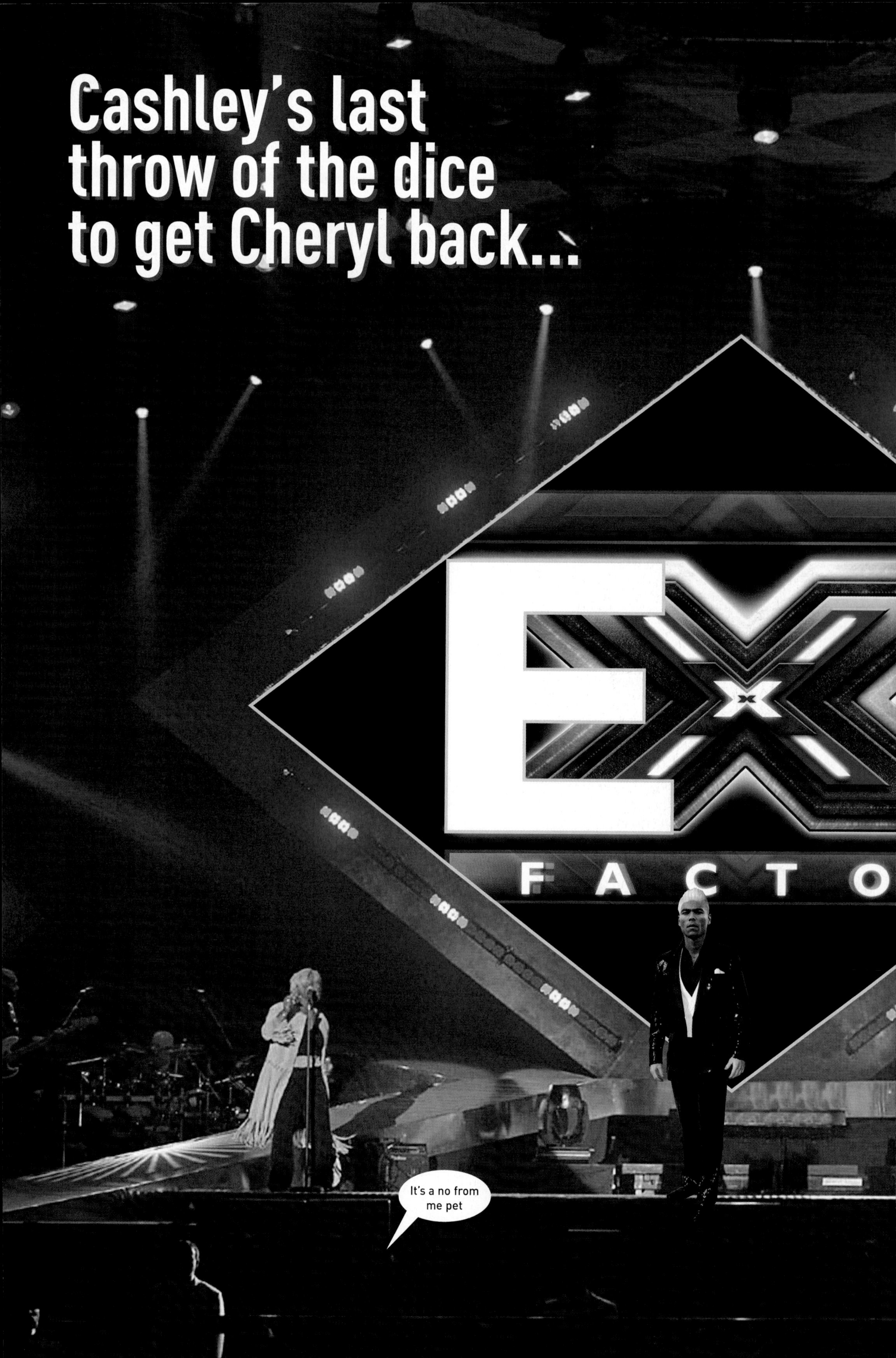

**And the other Chavski acts that didn't make it past the first audition...**

**Alex and a berk**

**Frank Waller**

**...and Ferreira and Hilario star as Deadwood**

THE KOP
CLASSIC POSTER

Standard Chartered

we've got the
BEST MIDFIELD
IN THE...

LUCAS

# ARRIVEDERCI

THANKS FOR MAKING MORE OF AN IMPRESSION THAN YOUR HUSBANDS DID

(No offence Diego, what could you do with Pepe ahead of you)

(Michela's fella though was like an Aqua Man out of water)

# EVERTON UNVEIL TIMELINE

TO try and brighten the old biddy, sorry, girl up, Everton have installed a photographic flatline, er, timeline around three sides of the outside of Goodison Park, which hilariously features an (already vandalised) image of Nick 'Judas' Barmby opposite the Winslow Hotel. To save you having to cross Stanley Park to see it, here is what we assume it looks like…

**1892:** Alcohol peddler John Houlding disgracefully forces us out of Anfield by upping the rent to a ludicrous level to feather his dirty Redsh*te nest

**1928:** Dixie Dean scores 60 league goals in the same season including three against the Redsh*te at Anfield

**1953:** Everton are promoted to the First Division and the Redsh*te are relegated to the Second Division

**1966:** Alan Ball turns down the Redsh*te to sign for Everton

**1977:** Clive Thomas denies Everton a place in the FA Cup final by scandalously disallowing a perfectly good goal against the Redsh*te at Maine Road

**1984:** Alan Robinson denies Everton the League Cup in the final at Wembley by failing to award a penalty against the Redsh*te's Alan Hansen for handball

**1985:** Everton are banned from Europe because of the Redsh*te

**1986:** Gary Lineker scores against the Redsh*te in the FA Cup final at Wembley to give Everton a 1-0 lead at half-time

**1989:** Stuart McCall heroically scores two equalisers against the Redsh*te in the FA Cup final at Wembley

**2000:** Graham Poll denies Everton a Merseyside derby win against the Redsh*te at Goodison by disallowing a perfectly good Don Hutchison goal because he'd blown the final whistle

**2002:** David Moyes puts those Redsh*te Norwegians in their place by pointing out that we are the People's Club

**2005:** Everton finish above the Redsh*ite in the Premier League and they get stuffed 3-0 in the first half of the Champions League final by AC Milan

**2005:** Redsh*te Pierluigi Collina denies Everton a place in the Champions League by disallowing a perfectly good Duncan Ferguson goal against Villarreal

**2007:** The Redsh*te are beaten 2-1 in the Champions League final in Athens by AC Milan, but then Mark Clattenburg turns us over in the Goodison derby

**2010:** The Redsh*te get rid of the Fat Spanish Waiter who spent £900 zillion more than David Moyes, who has never had any money ever

**2010:** The Redsh*te suffer their most embarrassing defeat in their history losing to a fourth division team as we out-do them by only go out to a third division side

# chants to tell the truth

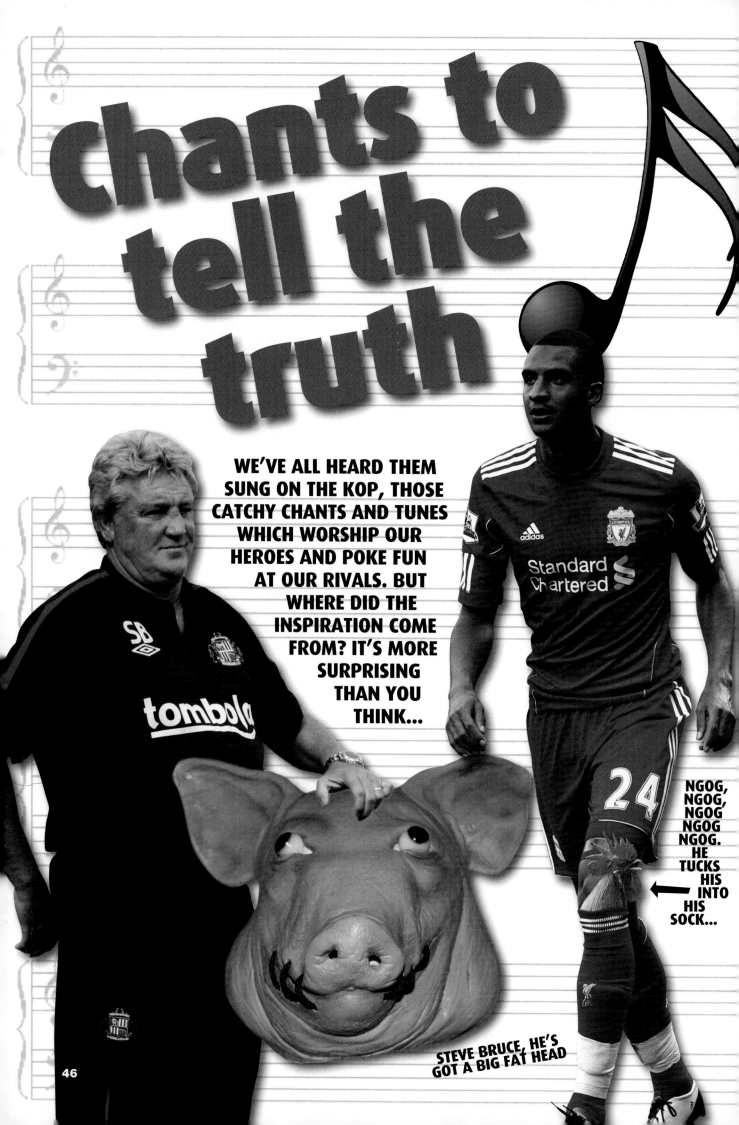

WE'VE ALL HEARD THEM SUNG ON THE KOP, THOSE CATCHY CHANTS AND TUNES WHICH WORSHIP OUR HEROES AND POKE FUN AT OUR RIVALS. BUT WHERE DID THE INSPIRATION COME FROM? IT'S MORE SURPRISING THAN YOU THINK...

NGOG, NGOG, NGOG NGOG NGOG. HE TUCKS HIS INTO HIS SOCK...

STEVE BRUCE, HE'S GOT A BIG FAT HEAD

IN FOR A WEEK, OUT FOR A MONTH

POOR SCOUSER TOMMY

BINMAN, WHAT'S
THE SCORE?

# chants to tell the truth

DIOUF, DIOUF, DIOUF IS ON FIRE

Welcome to MANCHESTER
www.mcfc.co.uk

OH MANCHESTER IS FULL OF...

RAFA'S GOT HIS DIRK OUT

BENNY IS A DANCER

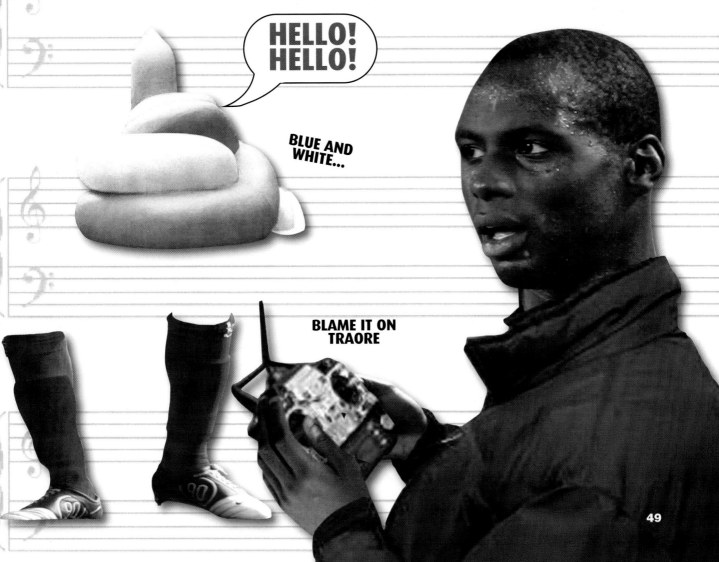

49

## GOIN' UNDERGROUND

WHICH former Liverpool player refused to give interviews to club media because they stopped ringing him last season as all he ever wanted to talk about was why Rafa Benitez should be sacked?

## WHAT'S OCCURRING WITH STEVIE?

SINCE Peter Crouch left Liverpool a lot of Kopites have felt we've needed a big man to play ahead of Steven Gerrard, but James Corden wasn't exactly what they had in mind. The Gavin and Stacey star turned up in Southport this year at the Warehouse Kitchen and Bar launch – which Stevie co-owns. Rafa Benitez was unable to attend the evening, which was a shame as he and Corden, who played Smithy in the BBC comedy, have something in common – things went badly wrong when they got involved with Barry.

## TV TWEET

ONE Liverpool player has generously given a TV to club physios.

"New 42' inch TV in the physio room," tweeted Chris Morgan, the Reds physio who tweets under the name 'morg_morg' on Twitter.

"Hayley McQueen on Sky Sports News = never seen the physio room so full!"

So that's where Fabio Aurelio's been...

# THE KOP MOLE

*With the EXCLUSIVE news from 2010*

## No thanks, Djimi

I KNOW things are on the expensive side in Monaco, but it seems things in the millionaire's playground have reached ridiculous levels.

On a recent trip to the Principality, a couple of Kop readers discovered that Monaco's club shop wanted 70 Euros (just over £60) for a Djimi Traore replica shirt!

Funnily enough there wasn't a queue to buy them.

## Itandje enjoys his hard-earned wages

CHARLES Itandje continues to linger around Liverpool like a bad smell.

Dining with a female friend in the swanky San Carlo restaurant on Castle Street, his drink-ordering technique was as bad as his goalkeeping.

As the waiter walked past he abruptly, and rather rudely, said "wine" and pointed to the table.

The day when someone points Itandje towards the exit door and says "go" can't come soon enough.

## Europa League lapping up business

LIVERPOOL'S failure to qualify for the Champions League has cost the club millions and it is being claimed that it could play a part in putting city centre lapdancing bars out of business!

The smoking ban and the recession have already seen a drop in trade and, according to the boss of two local lappies, the number of Reds home games switched to Sundays because of the Europa League and Sky is also causing a major problem.

"Business is dead everywhere," John Fox, owner of Angels on Cumberland Street and VIP on Old Hall Street, told the Liverpool ECHO.

"At the moment we specialise in stag dos, but without that it is the football crowd. With matches regularly changed to Sundays, that trade has dried up." If only Liverpool had signed a couple of different Chavski players instead of Joe Cole, business would be booming.

## Now digging out even more Kop goss and dishing even more dirt on our rivals!

Follow us at twitter.com/thekopmagazine

MAKING arrangements to look after the kids while they're on their school holidays is something every parent has to sort out and it's no different for Liverpool's players.

Quite a few of them brought their youngsters down to Melwood while they were training during the Easter break with some rather funny consequences.

Jamie Carragher's lad James was overheard asking a member of the press 'what yer doin?' while another player I won't name had to be called in off the training pitch after his child complained of being frightened by one of his team-mate's kids!

Sounds like they need a Kindergarten Kop down there...

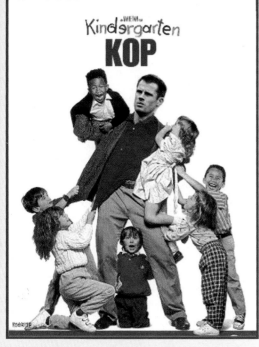

**WIFE-EYE**

BECAUSE YOU CAN'T TRUST ANY MALE

## HOTEL PLAYA WAY
### OFFICIAL WORLD CUP HOTEL OF TEAM ENGLAND

# WAGS PUT THEIR HEELS DOWN OVER ENGLAND STARS' HOTEL

**Wives and girlfriends of national squad insist team stay in WIFE-EYE enabled hotel in future with 'broads banned' technology**

*Cameras installed in players' hotel rooms with Chavski WAGs requesting extra measures to ensure privacy for their partners*

**Capello steps in to stop WAGs interfering with Rooney's suite claiming he doesn't want star player distracted and 'there's no point'**

**WIFE-EYE**

BECAUSE YOU CAN'T TRUST ANY MALE

Customer testimony: *'I was married to a footballer. When I suspected his groin strains weren't picked up on the pitch I had WIFE-EYE put in his hotel room. Next day he turned up for training with a smashed kneecap. Thank you WIFE-EYE'*

# TAXI FOR BABEL
## ...TO WASHINGTON NICK!

**HEARD** the one about the Liverpool player who fell asleep in a taxi, refused to pay the fare after the driver tried to rip him off and got taken to the Police station only to be released because the officer who dealt with him was a Red?

If not then you clearly don't follow Ryan Babel on Twitter.

The Reds winger and the rest of the Dutch team were banned from Tweeting during the World Cup, but after the tournament he was as prolific as ever and in July he told his followers about his rather strange experience in a taxi in Washington DC.

So here, in full, including plenty of slang and some rather bad grammar, is Ryan Babel's unedited true story of how a 10 minute journey in the American capital turned into a seven hour nightmare...

@RyanBabel So I'm waiting on Washington for a taxi right .. And one stops. It was like a big taxi van .. It had like 3 rows where u could sit .. So I'm jumping in all the way in the back .. I gave him the address where I needed to be it suppose to be a drive for like 10 min max ...

I was kinda tired so I closed my eyes hoping dat the driver would give me a shout when we were there .. So I'm sleeping rite .. And the next thing u know .. After 5 min drive he stops for 2 pretty lady's who were waiting for a taxi too

He asked where they needed to go ... "To the airport" Pretty lady's : "we r in a hurry so we need to go to the airport asap, can u take us" So the driver said of course I can take u guys jump in .. I was still sleeping .. While this happened

Next thing I know .. I woke up .. Looked outside and saw dat we were driving 70 miles n hour on the motor way ..

I screamed to the driver .. : Hey what the hell .. Where we going .. ????? At the same time the girls were looking both to the bak and .. And where shocked cause they didn't knew there was a guy sleeping in the back .. Pretty girls : Who the hell r u?????? What's going on here .. Driver hellooo who is dis guy???

The driver was so embarrassed .. He totally forgot he had a passenger in the back sleepin .. He totally for got me ..He apologized constantly .. And said sorry sorry .. I bring them quik to the airport then I will bring u back ..So I looked at the girls like what's goin on here .. The girls looked at me like what the hell is disss ...

When we dropped the girls .. We drove back to where I needed to be .. When we were at the destination .. The counter was on $68,50

I looked at the driver I said how much do I need to pay now???? Cause I aint gonna pay dat ..By the way the driver I think was a pakistan kinda guy (I think ) He said uhmm .. Give me 20 .. I said: WHAT ... R u nuts ..This drive suppose to be 6, 7 doller max .. 20 dollers????? Hell nooo He was like yes yes ..I want 20 dollars.. He was like arguing with me ..

So after 5 min arguing.. Left 8 dollar on the seats and walked out ..Next thing u know .. He stepped out his car and starts screaming : GIVE ME MY MONEY !!!!! GIVE ME MY MONEY !!!

Everybody was looking at me like .. Dude r u serious u didn't payed him ???? I try to walk away quickly.. Next thing .. Police on a motor cycle .. Stopped me .. What a coincidence ..

Police: Where do u think u going with out paying the tax driver ???? I looked at the police dude .. And was thinking : What's is going to happen now .. #jail??? nahh nahh .. Can't be ..Me the police and the driver where arguing on about what happend...

Ok dat didn't worked .. I had to go the police station .. 10 min away after he heard I was from Holland ..I brought my passport with me .. And they were askin me questions like .. Why u here for what am I doin bak home etc etc Next thing u know .. Police said .. : why looks ur name so familiar???? And he starts lookin at me ..

Yes officer .. I play football ... Officer: American football???? Noo sorry my bad.. I play soccer ..where do u play??? I play for Liverpool fc sir .. His face starts changing and he starts .. Noooo wayyyyy??? LIVERPOOL???? IM a MASSIVE LFC FAN ...

Next thing .. He is talking so longgg about last season .. About the bad year ..and everything ... Same story ... Then at the end he was like : ur free to go man, good luck for next season .. I was like ok thanks .. Wat about the taxi driver????? Officer: ahh don't worry about dat .. We take care of dat ..

I'm finally on my destination .. At 830pm... I took the taxi at 1.20pm All day wasted .. While the the journey should have bin 10 min max !!!!! Can u believe dat????? The End !!!

Zzzzz...

A long-running mystery was finally solved in 2010. It came as a big shock to us as the Stig we knew rarely ever got into Top Gear

# THE STIG'S SECRET IDENTITY FINALLY REVEALED

Inge Bjornebye: Drove us all mad

# IN OUR EVERPOOL HOME

■ A Local business consortium, the Mersey Stadia-Connex Group, recently unveiled proposals for a 'siamese stadium' to house both Liverpool and Everton. The clubs rejected the idea out of hand, but with both the Reds and Blues short of transfer funds, The Kop can exclusively reveal that next season they will introduce 'siamese players' who will appear for both sides. A joined spokesman said: "Dirk Neville will be a big hit with the ladies."

## Tony Degen

**Position: Right back**

**Most likely to:** Get beaten by a winger, get injured, get stick from the crowd

**Least likely to:** Play well, score, be a fans' favourite

## Marouane Skrtel

**Position: Treatment Room**

**Most likely to:** Clash heads with Jamie Carragher or legs with Soto Kyrgiakos

**Least likely to:** Fight over the shampoo in the shower after the match

## Dirk Neville

**Position: Defence/midfield/attack (Rafa Moyes' kind of player)**

**Most likely to:** Score a great glancing header at the Annie Road End on derby day, perform a kung-fu challenge on, er, himself

**Least likely to:** Have a popular brother, win a beauty contest, get dropped

# REVEALED – NEW EVERPOOL BOSS:

What do you get if you cross David Moyes with Roy Hodgson?

+

=

Hmm...

August saw a flurry of transfer activity with no fewer than 21 players leaving by the end of the window, while Hodgson boosted our homegrown quota with Brad Jones and Paul Konchesky, and our Masch-less midfield with Christian Poulsen and Raul Meireles. In truth, though, Hicks' 'big' summer never transpired as he kept 'his' money in his pockets ... and his hands in his trousers

# Jamie Carragher
# My WORLD CUP in pictures

BETWEEN INTERNATIONAL RETIREMENTS JAMIE CARRAGHER PLAYED IN THE 2010 WORLD CUP. WE ALL KNOW YOU CAN'T BELIEVE WHAT YOU READ IN THE TABLOIDS SO CARRA TELLS THE KOP ANNUAL WHAT THE ENGLAND SQUAD REALLY SAID AND DID WHILE THEY WERE AWAY WHICH LED TO THEIR ULTIMATE FAILURE

*Why would Carra wanna play for Capello?*

*Must be worse than playin for Rafa*

It all started towards the end of the 2009/10 season when Stevie told me to expect a call from Fabio Capello...

I knew it could be my last chance at a World Cup and I wanted to see what Capello was like as a manager so I got on the plane to South Africa and in my press conference I even said all the right things about wanting to play for the *wonderful* England fans...

The spirit in the camp was high, especially when Stevie scored first against the USA. I got on the pitch too and managed to take out some of my Yank frustration on some of their players...

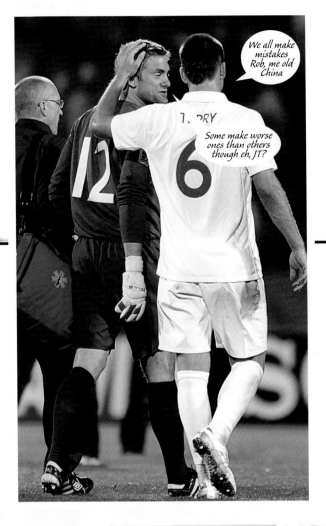

But when Rob Green's error led to us only drawing our opening game, things started to unravel...

Fabio gave Rob some self-help tapes to listen to to help him regain his confidence but he could barely hear them over the sound of Frank Lampard Jr drooling every time we went past a McDonalds...

Some of the lads were pretty happy in training but it didn't help the way some of them reacted when they watched Emile Heskey in shooting practice...

And I must admit that even I started to wonder why some of the lads were there in the first place. They seemed to hand out a team suit to anyone...

In the next game the Algerians couldn't believe how bad we were, and back at the hotel we were kept awake all night by people who'd been the game trying to claim a refund...

# Jamie Carragher
# My WORLD CUP in pictures

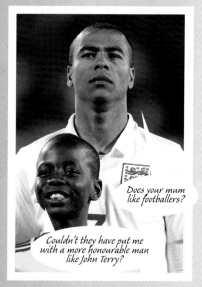

*Does your mum like footballers?*

*Couldn't they have put me with a more honourable man like John Terry?*

*Midnight feast in my room tonight...*

As the pressure mounted on the players, some of them started to revert to type...

*So, errr, JT. Is there anyone in Row X whose phone number you haven't got?*

And even though we managed to beat Slovenia to qualify for the knockout phase, some players started to form cliques and take the p*** out of each other...

*Psst, Stevie, look at the sticker on the boss' back. He he...*

*Very funny Frank, but how can you call anyone else FLABio?*

*Ledley King plays more games than you, yer crock!*

*Martin Luther King plays more than you, yer panty-wearing weirdo*

The criticism of our poor performances hit Wayne particularly hard. He went off the rails a bit and even got a tattoo without asking Coleen...

I'll have the banquet for five on one plate

And when the media criticism of Wayne reached its peak, he hit the bottle (of HP sauce). The calls started going in to local takeaways with alarming regularity, so Stevie had to play a captain's role and confiscate Rooney's phone...

How many times have you scored from your own half?

I can't believe you Cameron! Why would you wanna take away the free bus pass for pensioners?

I even found myself struggling to concentrate in training and the eventual loss to Germany was no real surprise. Everyone thought Wayne was annoyed that the linesman didn't spot Lampard's shot had gone over the line but he actually flipped when he saw Britain's new Prime Minister in the crowd and wanted to confront him about an issue close to his heart...

Do you know if there are any jobs going at Alitalia?

Christine looks different without her make-up

Can I come back with you Carra?

It all meant an early flight home and everyone felt terrible about how we'd played. Everyone felt like we'd let the nation down. It felt like the end of the world to everyone...except me. I knew I'd be up in the car to Liverpool where no-one could give a monkey's about England. Three Lions...nah, five times more like it

# London's
## Champions League
## Winners
# Roll Of Honour

(Updated version 2010)

*You Ask, We Answer*

HAVING grown my hair for a number of years, I recently decided that I'd like to have it styled in a fashion that gets the birds to notice me because I'm single.

So I went into my local hairdressers and asked for a 'Fellaini cut', to which the barber obliged.

I can confirm that this did indeed attract the birds and I soon became acquainted with some Great Tits, which are now nesting in my barnet.

*Herr Cutneeded,
Germany*

**A: Fellaini's hair has also attracted a lot of blue tits to Goodison Park.**

I AM writing to complain about the sick chant I heard made by Liverpool supporters during the Manchester City game at Eastlands this season.

I viewed the game on Sky TV and clearly heard the Liverpool fans chant 'oh Joleon Lescott, the elephant man'.

For them to draw such a disgusting comparison with such an unfortunately disfigured individual sickened me and I believe a full apology is in order.

*The Elephant Man, London*

**A: Sadly you have experienced the ugly side of football.**

I BUMPED into a Jari Litmanen lookalike in our local newsagents. He was buying 20 Benson & Hedges and a packet of extra strong mints. Do I win a prize?

*Brian Straw-Clutcher,
Hants*

**A: Are you the one making the silent phone calls?**

AS a regular viewer of Sky Soccer Saturday I am puzzled by the choice of 'experts' they employ.

Dean Windass sounds thicker than the fog on the Yorkshire Moors, Charlie Nicholas still hasn't worked out that just because he's wearing headphones doesn't mean people can't hear him, and Chris Kamara can tell you what's happening without looking at the pitch.

When are Sky going to stop employing these buffoons and

give us true experts who know the game and can get their points across in an eloquent manner?

*Rodney Marsh, Herts*

**A: Are you trying to say Phil Thompson isn't eloquent?**

EVERYBODY knows about Alex Ferguson giving his players the hairdryer treatment, but my mate reckons that the red nosed gum-chewing stop-watch checker is a bit partial to it himself.

He even claims that Fergie travels to a local school every month for a quick blow dry as it's cheaper than going to a swanky salon on Deansgate!

So please can you tell me if Slur Alex enjoys the hairdryer treatment, or is my mate just off his head?

*Kenny Believeit,
Glasgow*

**A: Your mate is indeed correct, and therefore on his head, as our picture shows.**

I WAS at Middlesbrough's Riverside Stadium on the opening day of the 1996/97 season when Liverpool drew 3-3.

Stig Inge Bjornebye scored that day but this unusual event was overshadowed by a hat-trick for Boro's new Italian striker Fabrizio Ravanelli.

That night they were all raving about him on Match of the Day, but I believe to this day that the BBC covered-up what happened after his third goal.

I can clearly recall Ravanelli stripping down to his underpants and threatening to take them off until a team of stewards apprehended the greying striker and carried him off the

pitch and all the way to a police station in Redcar.

I realise this was a long time ago, but would you be able to confirm that this incident isn't just in my imagination?

*Trev Lingred, Rainhill*

**A: Hopefully the above picture strips away the doubts.**

For the last 46 years a signed photograph of Elisha Scott, the legendary Northern Irish custodian, has taken pride of place on my mantlepiece and been a conversation starter on many occasions during visits from friends and relatives.

I now wish to auction off this prized possession as it has been pointed out to me that Scott played 468 games for Liverpool, an upsetting revelation for a life-long Evertonian such as myself.

*Gwladys Street,
Wales*

**A: A sad end to a beautiful glove afair.**

AFTER taking my girlfriend out for a sumptious meal, plying her with fine wine and lavishing her with expensive gifts, imagine my delight when we arrived home and she told me to go and wait in the bedroom while she slipped into something a little more racy.

Unfortunately things didn't work out as planned as I'd over-looked the fact that we live next door to John Terry and I've not seen her since she got into his Ferrari.

*W.B, Surrey*

**A: You should be able to track her down by reading the Sunday papers.**

CAN anyone explain to me why during the Blackpool game at Anfield the club employed 3,000 stewards and gave them all a seat in the away end?

I'm all for safety at football matches, but this seemed a little excessive and to then see them joyously jumping about in their orange coats when Blackpool scored their two goals while their mates are telling us to sit down on the Kop was outrageous.

*Taff Tasabrush,
Swansea*

**A: Never mind stewards, are you stupid?**

I WISH to call into question a Kop cahnt about the famous Bill Shankly.

According to the song, Bertie Mee said to Bill Shankly "have you heard of the North Bank Highbury?"

Shanks said "No, I don't think so, but I've heard of the Annie Road aggro."

I've always taken what the Kop sings as gospel, but having conducted some extensive research I believe that the aforementioned conversation never took place and the chant is simply a fabricated story by Liverpool fans to make the Anfield Road end look better than the North Bank.

*Eimar Bitslow,
Litherland*

**A: It appears that the Kop's support for Shankly is somewhat lost on you.**

I AM a Blackburn Rovers supporter who attended the 1994 Coca Cola Cup match against Liverpool at Ewood Park which was won 3-1 by the Reds due to an Ian Rush hat-trick.

During the course of the match a section of the Liverpool supporters began to chant "where were you when you where shit?"

That got me scratching my head for a few years but I am pleased to say that I can now answer the question.

I was in fact anywhere but Ewood Park because we were shit. The reason I can now remember this is becuase that is where you would have found me every weekend since 1996 as we are indeed shit again.

Should things change under

Sam Allardyce and his attractive brand of football I will once again return to Ewood Park and be happy to try and answer any further questions posed by inquisitive Scousers.

*G. L. Rory Hunter, Blackburn*

**A: Many thanks for the swift response to our query.**

IS it true that former Prime Minister Gordon Brown lost the general election for Labour because he wanted to make Arsene Wenger his Foreign Secretary?

If so then it shows just how stupid Mr Brown was as everybody knows that Mr Wenger's foreign policy hasn't been successful for years and he is clueless when it comes to Europe.

*Milly Band, Doncaster*

**A: As our picture shows, Mr Brown was indeed lining Wenger up for the job but he didn't see the General Election defeat coming.**

I'VE read so many things about Rafa Benitez's departure from Liverpool FC that I don't know what to believe.

Some people say he was forced out by Christian Purslow, others reckon the players wanted rid of him and there have been stories that the board were not prepared to give him any more transfer funds after

wasting so much on bad players.

There are even people who reckon Rafa himself was fed up working under the constraints put on him by Tom Hicks and George Gillett so resigned.

So what is the truth? Was Rafa pushed or did he jump?

*Bob Syeruncle, Tuebrook*

**A: The truth is that Rafa Benitez was fired for gross misconduct after doing an impression of a teapot on the touchline at St Andrews and poking Alex McLeish in the nose. As you can see from our picture, the evidence is damning.**

I'M just writing to thank Liverpool Football Club for helping us to have our most successful free advertising campaign ever.

With LFC ending up in the Europa League twice in quick succession, we now have people up and down the country singing about us being THE channel to watch on a Thursday night.

Hopefully it'll be a long time before people realise most of Liverpool's Europa League games are screened on ITV and ESPN.

*Richard Desmond, Channel Five*

**A: Manish Bhasin is hoping Liverpool get relegated so "Football League Show, Saturday Night" gets an airing next year.**

## KOP TIPS ... KOP TIPS ...

**\* Brought to you in association with the two stewards who race to stand next to the goalposts in front of the Kop for no apparent reason when Liverpool score**

\* NEMANJA Vidic – remember to set Sky+ to record the Liverpool v Manchester United game in March so you can see how it finishes for a change.

**Matt Choficial, Anfield**

\* AWAY fans – instead of singing 'shall we sing a song for you?' when visiting Anfield, why not just go ahead and do it anyway because we couldn't give a flying one if you do or don't.

**Seamus Kopites, Liverpool 4**

\* SAVE Alex Ferguson the travel expenses associated with making a journey to the Vatican City by visiting England to tell him that you still don't know who the fuck Man United are.

**Joseph Ratzinger, Rome**

\* WHEN you walk through a storm, hold your head up high and don't be afraid of the dark as this is likely to have been caused by a shadow from the umbrella you are holding.

**Gerry Marsden, Toxteth**

\* GET yourself several weeks worth of free national newspaper advertisements for the discreet personal services you offer by sleeping with a married Shrek look-a-like seven times for £1,200 a night.

**Jennifer Thompson, Bolton**

\* QUESTION the selection of one of Liverpool's central midfielders by chanting 'Lucas Leiva, Lucas Leiva, ay, ay?' during matches.

**Fay Muskopite, Garston**

\* MAKE a financial killing by charging Liverpool fans over the odds for Anfield match breaks safe in the knowledge that they'll be prepared to pay it because they can't get tickets any other way.

**Thomas Cook, High Street**

\* GOSSIP mongers - before starting vicious rumours about a footballer allegedly having an affair with his sister-in-law, check that

his wife actually has a sister.

**May Dupbyblues, Walton**

\* KIDS – take the advice of Ian Rush and drink lots of milk. I certainly wish I had.

**Ray Putterill, Accrington**

\* GIVE your husband an ideal excuse to force through a transfer to a warmer climate by refusing to learn the language of the country you're in and living like a hermit.

**Mrs Mascherano, Barcelona**

\* ABBEY Clancy – ensure that Peter Crouch doesn't stray again by asking him to get a move to Hull City. The women are so rough nobody pays for it up there.

**Ad Vicegal, London**

\* GET the Yanks out by asking the Vietnam branch of the supporters club to run the campaign against them. They'll eventually realise it's a battle they can't win.

**Cameron Bodia, Asia**

\* FOOTBALLERS - employ a body double to take medicals for you, thus fooling a club considering offering you a contract into thinking you're fully-fit when in fact you'll pick up more injuries than Whiston Hospital's A&E sees in a year.

**Fabio, Anfield**

\* LADIES - don't listen to the chant Liverpool fans used to sing about Duncan Ferguson when it happens to be 'that time of the month' as it can lead to painful consequences.

**Claire Rayner, out for a month**

\* CHRISTIAN Poulsen - try running around and closing down opponents during a game. Then you'll feel like you're doing the job you're being paid to do.

**Anne Greebird, Fazakerley**

\* DELIA Smith - make Norwich City rich again by flogging club scarves outside Old Trafford on match days to dumb Mancs who think they're getting one over on Malcolm Glazer.

**Sue Veneer, Salford**

# The best of SPOTTED

**Driving in-range: Didi Hamann plays golf near Lord Cisse's Manor, and shops in WH Smiths**

**John Barnes** in furniture store Chateaux in Chester on the day of the Atletico Madrid away game.

**Jennifer Ellison** getting into a white Land Rover outside the passport office on Old Hall Street the day after Liverpool's 4-0 away win over Burnley.

**Dean Bouzanis** walking past Subway on Exchange Street East the day before the Atletico home game.

**Paolo Di Canio** getting into a taxi outside the Radisson, Old Hall Street, on the afternoon of the Atletico semi-final second leg.

**Roy Evans** chatting with Rangers boss **Walter Smith** in the Anfield directors box before the Atletico match kicked off.

**Dave Kirby** stood in flagpole corner before the Chavski match.

**Ronnie Moran** driving through Formby Village.

Featherweight boxer **Stephen Smith** playing football at Powerleague a few days after the Chavski game.

A hooded **Sotirios Kyrgiakos** going into Prima Master dry-cleaners with a couple of bags full of clothes on Old Hall Street on the day of the General Election.

**Sammy Lee** leaving the Bishop Eton Church Hall polling station in Woolton.

**Dirk** and **Gertrude Kuyt** arriving at San Carlo for tea shortly after the Gerrards had left.

**Robbie Fowler** posing for pictures with Kopites at John Bishop's Liverpool ECHO Arena gig.

**Jamie Carragher** driving down Lydiate Lane on the night of Liverpool's 0-0 draw at Hull.

**Steven Gerrard** with his family in the Emirates Business Lounge at Birmingham Airport before boarding a flight to

**Unlucky limo: Jen Metcalfe swaps vehicles**

Dubai and taking the 25-minute bus ride from Dubai Airport to the terminal the day after the Hull game.

Jermaine Pennant's ex-girlfriend **Jennifer Metcalfe** sat in a limo outside the Registry Office in Liverpool.

**David Fairclough** signing copies of Chris McLoughlin's Spion Kop book at Pritchards Books in Formby.

**Didi Hamann** driving in the direction of Frodsham Golf Club, near to Djibril Cisse's manor house.

**Matt Littler** and **Darren Jefferies** (formerly Max and OB in Hollyoaks) leaving a flat on Bold Street.

**Rick Parry** talking on his phone and wearing a garish shirt as he walked past the Disney Shop in Liverpool One.

**Jennifer Metcalfe** again, now getting out of a white Audi on Lark Lane the day before the Europa League final.

Most Haunted's paranormal investigator **Ciaran O'Keeffe** buying a ticket at London Euston station.

TV presenter **Jenny Powell** stood outside Sainsbury's, Old Hall Street.

**Alex Curran** driving a black Bentley down Heathfield Road, Ainsdale.

**Gin & Tonic: Sammy Lee loves it**

The Coral's **James Skelly** having a meal in La Vina the night before the Champions League final.

**Sammy Lee** enjoying a gin and tonic or two on the afternoon of Blackpool's Play-off victory, at the Bear and Staff pub in Gateacre Village.

**Daniel Agger** chatting with friends in Danish stood near the LFC club shop in Liverpool One (Everton nil).

**Jay Spearing** with a female companion on a train down to London to watch the Black Eyed Peas and Cheryl Cole at the O2 Arena.

Ex-Man City winger **Dennis Tueart** leaving the Odeon cinema in the Trafford Centre shortly after a punch-up erupted inside.

**Didi Hamann** with his family in the WH Smith inside Terminal One at Manchester Airport.

**Craig Johnston** walking through Hyde Park, London, on the day Rafa Benitez lost his job.

Olympic gymnast **Beth Tweddle** going into Marks & Spencer at Speke Retail Park.

**Michael Shields** walking down Tithebarn Street with the morning papers tucked under his arm on the day the World Cup kicked off.

Reds supporting jockey **Franny Norton** celebrating his 40th

The Kop Mole has got spies all over the place and nothing escapes his watchful eye. From a Sammy Lee drinking session to Nathan Eccleston's dodgy cardie to our Danish defender Daniel Agger speaking Danish . . . here's a few GENUINE sightings from the past year!

**Shoppers: Carly Cole and family spotted in Zara**

birthday in Gusto, Albert Dock (Michael Owen was on the guest list but I don't know if he showed up).

**Carly Cole** with her mum and baby Ruby shopping in Zara Home, Liverpool One.

**Christian Purslow** leaving Café Connect on Old Hall Street clutching what suspiciously looked like a tall latte on the day before the Rabotnicki away game.

**Fernando Torres** on the beach at Formentara, Spain, with wife Olalla and daughter Nora. Reserve striker **Nicola Saric** walking down Castle Street wearing a black t-shirt with a gun on it on the same day.

**Sotirios Kyrgiakos** going into Sainsbury's, Old Hall Street, the day after the Borussia Moenchengladbach friendly.

**Marouane Fellaini** wearing a green hoodie over his afro

and reading magazines in Tesco, Old Hall Street, on the day of their friendly v Everton Chile.

**Dr Peter Brukner** walking past the passport office in Liverpool City Centre on the morning after the home win against Rabotnicki.

**Joe Cole** taking stick from Newton Heath fans on a London Euston to Liverpool train after the Community Shield at Wembley.

**Dani Pacheco** sat in a taxi outside La Vina, North John Street, for ages before finally getting out and going into the restaurant.

**Nathan Eccleston** wearing a dodgy cardigan in Nando's, Queen's Square, a couple of nights before the Arsenal match.

**Roy Hodgson** watching the Blackburn v Everton game at Ewood Park on the opening day of the season (and leaving early because it was so bad!)

**Lucas** being stopped to pose for photos and sign autographs near to John Lewis in Liverpool One.

Reds legend **David Johnson** sporting a new-look goatee beard in the Main Stand at the Arsenal match.

**Ronnie Moran** keeping himself fit by walking around the perimeter fence at Melwood.

**Franny Jeffers** being recognised by absolutely no-one as he walked through Liverpool One on a busy Wednesday afternoon.

**Roy Hodgson** having a meal with his wife in Quarter, off Hope Street, after the 1-0 victory over the Baggies.

**Jamie Carragher, Stephen Warnock,**

**Emile Heskey, David Thompson** and many others in Jury's Inn, Keel Wharf, after Carra's testimonial.

**Steven Gerrard** filming a new advert for Lucozade in the Radisson, Old Hall Street, four days before the Birmingham game.

**Paul Konchesky** clutching a Boots carrier bag and looking a bit lost walking down Church Street.

**Ryan Babel** in Bruschetta's Café, Hunts Cross, buying a latte the day before September's trip to Birmingham.

**Thomas Gravesen** and his porn-star wife Kira Eggers in Philpotts, Exchange Flags, the day after Liverpool v Steaua Bucharest.

**Roy Hodgson** buying three pairs of Farah trousers in TJ Hughes.

Sex and The City's **Kim Cattrall** having a meal in Prego, Liverpool One.

**Rangy model: Jennifer Ellison stepped into a white Range Rover and reserve striker Nicola Saric is spotted in possession of a gun (on his shirt)**

**Track-ed down: Joe Cole took flak on a train as Jay Spearing went to see Cheryl Cole... er Twee... er... Cheryl in concert**

CHRISTIAN POULSEN

Standard Chartered

28

we've got the BEST MIDFIELD IN THE...

A record number of Reds made their respective World Cup squads, with four making the final and Torres and Reina bringing home winners' medals. Gerrard and Mascherano would exit with crushing defeats, while Carra was already packed ... and made sure he had two vuvuzelas for the kids

The best of **Summer CHALLENGE**

*THE past year has been another great one for Kop Summer Challenge 5 entries. As usual, you've been to all four corners of the world with The Kop magazine, getting your photos taken, and sometimes you've found famous people to be pictured with. There are many great shots from ex-Reds to road signs, and from famous stadiums to some q-w-ality lookalikes. One fan even catches up with Albert Riera, but that sinking ship has sailed. Can anyone top this lot for next year? It's over to you...*

*The Kop*

*Magazine,*

*Liverpool*

YOU'D think Aldo would be happy enough with having his own page in The Kop but clearly it's not enough for the Reds legend as he gatecrashed the Summer Challenge 5. Again.

The Kop columnist was playing in a charity match in Dublin, so Carlow-based Reds Paul Deere and Shane Coakley (holding The Kop) donned their 1986 double-winning shirts and lined up for a five-fingered salute alongside him.

Unfortunately Newton Heath supporting photographer Keith Hutton missed Shane's five-fingered salute off the picture, although to be fair it's never easy to take a photo while eating a prawn sandwich and waving a Norwich City scarf at the same time. On the plus side we can't see him.

Aldo signed their copies of The Kop and Paul says that he was a true gentleman, sentiments that were confirmed to us by an Egyptian FIFA official in a yellow hat who first met John at the Ireland v Mexico World Cup game in 1994.

John's only goal for Ireland in the World Cup came against Mexico but the Mexican's won 2-1, although it was somewhat controversial of FIFA to decide the result on the comparative length of moustaches grown in the respective countries.

A similar contest in the women's World Cup finished 6-1 to the central Americans.

HAVING been taken to Anfield for the first time aged just six-months old by her now 90-year-old fanatical Kopite father Bill Devine, a life-long Red, Ann Mark spread the word in style when she visited Hungary, Croatia and Bosnia this summer.
Even more impressive, though, is the fact that rocks near Hungary's Lake Balaton show their support for Liverpool FC by giving five-fingered salutes of their own. The last rock to be seen celebrating the Reds 5th European Cup in such a fashion was called Sami Hyypia.

HIS hand got to the ball before Peter Shilton and now he's got it on The Kop.

There can only be one Diego Maradona and obviously he spends his days dressed in full Argentina kit wandering the streets of Buenos Aires posing for photographs because he's got nothing better to do.

At first we thought Kopite Paul Holliday may be giving a five-fingered salute next to a Maradona look-a-like, but that can't be the case as shortly after the photograph was taken the same bloke told Paul that he was calling him up for Argentina World Cup squad so it must have been him.

THERE'S nothing that the owners of magazines love more than seeing their product pictured in a place which has the name of their publication hidden within it's name.

For instance, those in charge of OK! Magazine love to see it pictured in BangkOK, executives at Heat magazine get goosebumps when it's spotted in Hampstead HEATh and West Ham owners David Sullivan and David Gold are delighted when one of their magazines makes it to Scunthorpe.

Here at The Kop we're no different, so when Kopite Mick Clememt toured African countries Namibia, Zambia and N'Zogbia and took the Kop Summer Challenge 5 in Swakopmund, we were overjoyed.

Located on the Skeleton coast of Namibia, which is presumably co-called because it's bone dry, Swakopmund was formed in 1892, the same year as Liverpool Football Club, although not because a bunch of tea-total Methodists wouldn't pay the rent.

Mick gave a five-fingered salute while on the roof of his Land Rover, which is not something you should try at home, particularly if you drive a convertible.

# Summer CHALLENGE

IT'S not very often that you bump into an ex-footballer-turned-film-star on holiday, but that's exactly what Kopite Alan Condon did when he visited Animal World in Florida.

The Walton-based Red even persuaded former Everton midfielder Peter Reid, who played Rafiki in The Lion King, to give a five-fingered salute.

Alan tells us that while he was proudly taking the Kop Summer Challenge 5, a load of kids were stood nearby laughing, presumably at Reidy's face.

It's thought that the former England midfielder was in Animal World to prepare himself for dealing with supporters of Stoke City, or a dressing room argument between Tony Pulis and James Beattie.

The Lion King has several connections with the world of football.

Former Watford Chairman Sir Elton John wrote five original songs for the animated movie and it ends with a big fight, just as most Millwall matches do.

FIVE Fingers Strand is obviously a rather appropriate place for Kopites to give a five-fingered salute, but Galway-based Reds Christine and Dave went a step further (away).

They took the Kop Summer Challenge 5 five miles away from Five Fingers Strand in front of a road sign that had Five Fingers Strand 5 on it, meaning this sentence now has five 5's in it, excluding the five 5's we've just mentioned and the two we've just used to tell you to exclude the previous two.

You'll also spot a bit of Gaelic on the sign and if you don't speak the language we can tell you that 'Cuig Mear' roughly translates as 'five fingers'. Incidentally, 'Cascarino' roughly translates as 'useless lump of crap'.

We've never been to Malin Head but if you ever eat out in Ireland then we can recommend getting a side order with your meal.

Gaelic bread – it's the future.

NOW here's a Liverpool fan who must be hard – he can make BA fly without a glass of milk laced with sleeping pills.

To be honest, we can quite understand why the A-Team hard-man always refused to get on a plane – calling the last place you visit before flying 'terminal' doesn't exactly fill you with confidence.

Captain Vaughan Sculthorpe flies planes for British Airways but before boarding this Boeing 737 to Malaga, presumably not to see Josemi, he took the Kop Summer Challenge 5.

The Liverpool fan is nicknamed 'Scully', but wasn't chosen to play the character of the same name in the 1984 TV series 'Scully' as the producers didn't make a pilot episode.

LUCAS Leiva, Lucas Leiva, ay, ay?

When season ticket holder of 35 years Mark Jones went on holiday in Turkey with son Luke he thought he spotted our Brazilian midfielder working as a restaurant manager.

But once it was established that he could carry a plate forward rather just sideways and failed to bring down any diners with a clumsy trip, they realised that the Paloma Pasha hotel in Ozdere was home of a Lucas look-a-like.

The man in question is Mehmet Bal, a Fenerbache fan, but he liked The Kop so much that he not only agreed to take the Summer Challenge 5 with the Rainford-based pair, he kept it so he could have a read!

Seeing how Liverpool have beaten Galatasaray, Besiktas and Trabzonspor over the years, it's no wonder he likes us.

Mehmet has promised put The Kop on display in the hotel if we print the pic-

ture, which is a great, great honour.

We're pleased about it too.

Turkey is a popular destination for Kopites to give five-fingered salutes for obvious reasons – it's cheap – but only 91 Liverpool supporters travelled to the away Europa League game in Trabzon.

With the Turkish club charging £44-a-ticket hardly anyone could afford to go, perhaps explaining why they're called Trabzonspoor. Or Twazbonspor, as Roy Hodgson was calling them.

FOLLOWING a stop in Antigua, Darren Sunley took The Kop Summer Challenge 5 – he also gave a five-fingered salute in front of the famous Chichen Itza temple in Mexico, which is used for one of the games in Gladiators.

When the temple was first constructed, one of the Mexican builders took his wife to the top and threw her off. He later admitted to police that he wanted tequila.

BILL Shankly once told Brian Reade that Gerry Byrne was his favourite Liverpool player of all time because: "He epitomised everything I wanted in football."

Gerry might not have given a five-fingered salute, but as he is holding his 1965 FA Cup winner's medal in one hand, and showing that the broken right collar-bone he played 87 minutes of that cup final victory over Leeds with is still in good nick, we'll let him off.

The Anfield legend was in his local, the Esplanade Club in Ryhl, when die-hard Reds Alun and Erik Lloyd took the Kop Summer Challenge 5.

Erik is holding Gerry's 1966 World Cup winners' medal, while Alun can be seen with an even more valuable piece of memorabilia, an edition of The Kop.

Despite being a right-footed left-back who scored an own goal in a 5-1 defeat at Charlton on his debut as a 19-year-old, Gerry went on to make 333 appearances for the Reds and was harder than Tommy Smith.

"I was only 15 and playing in a five-a-side game at Melwood," recalled Smithy on www.shankly.com.

"I nutmegged Gerry Byrne and scored and I was on top of the world. A couple of minutes later a ball dropped between us, I went to head it and Gerry headed me and I went down with a gashed eye.

"As I lay on the ground covered in blood, Bill Shankly strolled across, looked down at me and said: 'Lesson number one, never nutmeg Gerry Byrne son and think you can get away with it'".

WE'VE no idea who discovered this Thai island, but after many days struggling to think of what to call it he must have thought 'Phuket'.

Thailand's largest island was on one of the major trading routes between China and India, making it the place where Martin Broughton should have spent the summer so Kenny Huang and Subrata Roy could get their bids to him easily.

Instead he spent the summer in the UK, presumably because he's the chairman of BA and as everyone knows BA won't fly anywhere – unless you lace his milk with sleeping pills.

Phuket gained its wealth from tin and rubber although no-one there had the foresight to mix the two to create a baked beans container that prevents pregnancies.

Two Kopites who did make it to Phuket this summer were San Antonio based Keith Czelusniak and his son Paul and the pair took the Kop Summer Challenge 5 on the back of an elephant, like you do. Would riding elephants be allowed in the UK? Ivory much doubt it.

They say that 'an elephant never forgets' although as most of them don't have debit cards and PIN numbers to remember then how do they know for sure?

DISPLAYED in a glass case inside the Corinthians FC museum in Sao Paulo is Pele's shirt from the 1970 World Cup final.

It appears to be suspended in mid-air but when we contacted Pele to see how he keeps it up he simply offered us a packet of blue pills, providing we paid with Mastercard.

Dundalk-based Red Shane McDonnell had no problem keeping it up (The Kop that is) when he gave a five-fingered salute in front of Pele's shirt during a trip to Brazil.

IT'S the most dangerous road in the world, even more dangerous than Elland Road if you are Peter Ridsdale, and a place where only the brave, stupid or people fancying a quiet drive to La Paz dare to go.

Bolivia's Unduavi-Yolosa Highway, second cousin of Steve, is also chillingly known as the 'El Camino de la Muerte' (the Road of Death) due to the thousands of people that have died after plunging off it. The 40 mile-long pothole filled dirt track winds down 12,000ft, has no barriers and in some places is just three metres wide, which isn't enough for two Frank Lampards to pass never mind two cars. On the plus side, there aren't any speed cameras.

Despite the sheer drops to the Amazon jungle, hair-pin bends and sudden weather changes, the road is still used by local traffic and thrill-seeking nutters on mountain bikes, such as Kopite Darren Sunley.

The intrepid Red took the Kop Summer Challenge 5 shortly before going rapidly downhill, a lot like Liverpool are under Roy Hodgson who also needs to mind the drop. Reports have reached us that Wayne Rooney has expressed a wish to visit Bolivia to travel down the road as he enjoys mounting bikes.

Annoyingly, Alex Ferguson has never been for a drive down the Unduavi-Yolosa Highway, something we hope will change as it's the one road we'd be more than happy to see him use the hard shoulder on.

HAVING been banished from Anfield by Rafa Benitez and failing to turn up for pre-season training at Melwood on Roy Hodgson's first day as manager, it looked Albert Riera was going to be harder to track down than Raoul Moat.

Maybe Northumbria Police should have called Alan Beckwith in because the Kopite not only caught up with the wayward winger but persuaded him to pose for a Kop Summer Challenge 5 picture.

Riera was in Palma Airport awaiting an Easyjet flight to Liverpool, although it was hardly a surprise that he chose to travel by air as he made it very clear that he has an issue with sinking ships.

Albert didn't give a five-fingered salute but he was holding a large orange book, so that makes it ok. The (former) Spanish international claimed that Benitez's dialogue with the players was "practically nil" – a bit like the number of goals he scored in 09/10.

Riera's frustration was perhaps understandable as in the 45 games he started for Liverpool he was substituted in 36, leaving some Reds to claim that Benitez favoured certain players and brought others off whether they were playing well or not.

We put this suggestion to the new Inter Milan boss but he flatly denied it, shortly before programming the numbers 9, 11 and 15 into the fourth official's electronic board at the San Siro.

THE name Soccer City is somewhat misleading referring to a stadium rather than a City, although it isn't half as mis-leading as the title of the film Snatch.

Soccer City is Africa's biggest stadium and hosted Spain's World Cup Final triumph in July 2010.

The outside of the stadium was designed to look like an African pot, with a ring of lights running around the bottom of the structure to simulate fire underneath the pot. The architect was clearly thinking outside the springboks.

There was talk of the Reds new stadium on Stanley Park being designed to look like Scouse pot, but there were fears too many fans would start smoking the grass. Despite this, George Gillett and Tom Hicks still managed to make a hash of it.

Kopite Ian Livingston, who may have been known as Ian Meadowbank Thistle until 1995, took the Kop Summer Challenge 5 outside Soccer City on the day of South Africa's pre-World Cup friendly against Columbia.

## 2010 shorts

**January's** FA Cup exit to Reading was the third time in six seasons that Liverpool have been knocked out of the cup by a Championship side. The attendance of 31,063 was the lowest for an FA Cup match at Anfield since 28,126 turned up for the 7-0 win over Rochdale in 1996.

**February's** derby was Liverpool's 70th league win over Everton, the fourth time they've done the double over the Blues in the Premier League. It was also Liverpool's 1,300th league win at Anfield.

**The February** tie with Unirea was Liverpool's first ever Europa League game. It was also the first time Liverpool have played a game officiated with five officials.

**In** the 4-1 victory over Portsmouth, Martin Kelly became the 29th player used by Liverpool in the Premier League that season, equalling the club record. The 28 out-field players used in the league was the most since 1953/54 when we used 28 and went down!

**The** 3-0 win over Sunderland in March was the 36th con-secutive home game in which Liverpool scored, the second best run in the club's history.

**Ryan Babel** became the 11th Liverpool player to be sent off in European competition when dismissed against Benfica.

**Pepe Reina** made his 250th appearance for the Reds in Lisbon against Benfica.

**Rafa Benitez** met Birmingham for the 8th time in the league in April, and didn't win a single one, making them the only league side he faced that he didn't beat.

**Liverpool's** 10th European game against Benfica made them our most regular

## Kop Barfly quiz of the year

1. Who conceded a late penalty in the Reading replay?
2. Who scored Liverpool's first league goal of 2010?
3. And which player made their debut as a substitute in the same game?
4. Which team did we play on our return to Channel five?
5. Who did the Reds beat in their only away win in the 2010 half of the 09/10 season?
6. Which player joined Dinamo Moscow in January 2010 after 0 goals in 12 games last season?
7. What milestone did Dirk Kuyt achieve in the Merseyside derby in February?
8. Which former England striker's European goal record was surpassed by Steven Gerrard after his goal at Unirea?
9. And which player made his 100th appearance in the same fixture?
10. Which player missed a penalty against the Reds in March?
11. Who converted two penalties past the Reds in one match, but then missed one at the World Cup?
12. What was Fernando Torres' last act of the 09/10 season?
13. Against which team did Yossi Benayoun score his last Liverpool goal?
14. In the final game of the season at Hull, who made their 200th Liverpool appearance?
15. Which two players made the most appearances in the 09/10 season?
16. Which four teams did we complete league doubles over in the 09/10 season?
17. Where did Liverpool Reserves finish in the league?
18. How many Liverpool players at the time played in the World Cup (not just in the squad)?
19. How many goals did the Reds score in three 10/11 pre season friendly matches?
20. Which player followed in the footsteps of Antonio Nunez by having

**M R Hodgson, Anfield L4**

Licensed to win silverware, serve doubles and trebles and provide champagne football

## Answers

25. Bill Shankly
24. First career red card
23. Primetime
22. Danny Wilson
21. David Ngog
20. Milan Jovanovic
19. None
18. 10 - Gerrard, Agger, Kyrgiakos, Maxi, Kuyt, Skrtel, Carragher, Johnson, Torres, Mascherano,
17. Third, behind United and City
16. Bolton, Burnley, Everton, West Ham
15. Jamie Carragher and Dirk Kuyt
14. Dirk Kuyt
13. Atletico Madrid
12. A second goal against Benfica
11. Oscar Cardozo, Benfica and Paraguay
10. Wayne Rooney
9. Daniel Agger
8. Alan Shearer
7. Scored his 50th Liverpool goal
6. Andriy Voronin
5. Burnley
4. Unirea Urziceni
3. Maxi Rodriguez
2. Sotirios Kyrgiakos
1. Yossi Benayoun

his initial squad number changed before his first appearance?
21. Who scored Liverpool's first goal of the 10/11 season?
22. Which LFC British summer signing is classed as a foreign player in the new Premier League '25' rule?

23. Which channel broadcasted our tie at FK Rabotniki?
24. What first did Joe Cole 'achieve' in his league debut?
25. Which manager's record did Roy Hodgson beat with five wins in his first five European games?

Pepe Reina introduces his team-mates, on a stage in Madrid. God help his daughter when she grows up and gets married.

http://www.youtube.com/watch?v=mY8gKel sYDY&feature=related

Fans let Tom Hicks know exactly what they think of him as clearly as hopefully our debts will be

http://www.youtube.com/watch?v=RO55BazkiZ4

## 2010 shorts

European opponents alongside Chavski.

**Fernando Torres** became the first player to score twice in four consecutive home games in the club's entire history after his brace against Benfica.

**The 37,697** attendance at home to West Ham in 09/10 was the lowest in the PL since December 2004 when 35,064 saw a 1-1 draw with Portsmouth.

**David Ngog's** goal against the Hammers in April was the 100th the Reds have scored against West Ham in the league at Anfield. Rob Green's own goal was the first scored by an opposition goalkeeper at Anfield in a PL match.

**Alberto Aquilani** became the 5th player of the 09/10 season to create three goals in the same PL game at Burnley, who were only the second team to fail to score against the Reds in 09/10 along with Everton.

**Jack Robinson** became the club's youngest ever player aged just 16 years and 250 days old when he made his debut against Hull City.

**Roy Hodgson** became the first LFC boss to win his first five European games by beating Steaua Bucharest 4-1.

**Joe Cole's** goal after 26 seconds against Steaua was the quickest in Europe in LFC history, beating Phil Boersma's record of 57 seconds.

**Liverpool's** Carling Cup exit to Northampton was the first time the club had been beaten by a side from the fourth tier of English football in the competition and the Reds first ever penalty shoot-out defeat at Anfield.

**Due** to fixture changes and Europa League participation, Liverpool FC didn't play a single away game on a Saturday with a 3pm kick-off in 2010. Only two Anfield games kicked off at 3pm on a Saturday.

# GREAT BOOK OFFERS... IT'S NO JOKE!

LOYAL readers of The Kop Annual and Kop Magazine are guaranteed great savings on Liverpool FC books – and it's no wind-up!

As a special thank you to the thousands of fans who have bought The Kop this year, we have set up a Christmas Book Club.

That doesn't mean we'll all be sitting around in big woolly jumpers chatting about the latest Dan Brown while it's snowing outside.

What it does mean is that you'll get a whopping 20 per cent off the normal book price. This is almost certainly better value than getting it from that website named after a rainforest that you usually use.

To take advantage of any of the great books on the next few pages, just log on to www.merseyshop.com and use the code KOP10 before 31/12/2010 while stocks last. It's so easy even Jason McAteer wouldn't get confused. No KOP10 discount on our 'Other offers and packages' deals though, Martin Skrtel says so.

Every self-respecting Kopite gets a Liverpool book for Christmas so make it easy for yourself and save yourself a few bob.

All proceeds raised will go towards the Kop Christmas party ... unless our chief accountant says otherwise.

---

'PROOF THAT LIVERPOOL FANS ARE DIFFERENT TO THE REST'
– The Liverpool Echo

## OH I AM A LIVERPUDLIAN AND I COME FROM THE SPION KOP

RRP: £8.99   **KOP10** Price: £7.19

JUST mention the name and it inspires images of colour, passion and spine-tingling excitement. This book captures the moments that made this unique enclosure a sporting phenomenon.

Anfield stars of past and present, managers, some of the great characters of the game and the fans themselves relive their memories and stories of the unique stand.

This new paperback edition of Oh I Am A Liverpudlian and I Come From The Spion Kop has been revised and updated with twice the amount of material as appeared first time around. It has been published to commemorate the 110th anniversary of the Battle of Spion Kop, which the Kop was named after.

**Call 0845 143 0001 or visit www.merseyshop.com**

---

RRP: £9.99   **KOP10** Price: £7.99

IAN CALLAGHAN is the record appearance maker for Liverpool Football Club.

Cally wore a Liver bird on his chest a remarkable 857 times during 18 years at the club.

Over the past 50 years he has been constantly involved with the club and is able to recount a host of inside stories about Merseyside's biggest football team. Cally On The Ball is easy to read and modestly priced for a hardback and will make an ideal gift book for all Liverpool fans, especially the older generation.

**Call 0845 143 0001 or visit www.merseyshop.com**

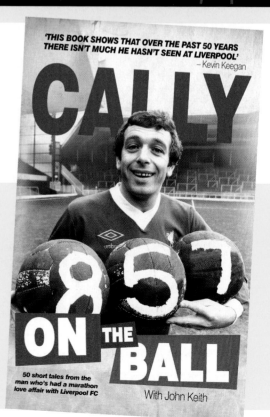

'THIS BOOK SHOWS THAT OVER THE PAST 50 YEARS THERE ISN'T MUCH HE HASN'T SEEN AT LIVERPOOL'
– Kevin Keegan

## CALLY 857 ON THE BALL

50 short tales from the man who's had a marathon love affair with Liverpool FC

With John Keith

RRP: £14.99

**KOP10** Price: £11.99

ALDO - aka John Aldridge - is the former Liverpool Football Club and Republic of Ireland striking legend who travels all over Europe following the fortunes of his beloved boys in red and green during his media work.

In 'Alright Aldo', the proud Irish Scouser draws on years of experience to produce a book that is full of hilarious inside stories.

From Anfield to Dublin, Newport to the Mexico World Cup and Istanbul to Cardiff, Aldo relives the funny side of being a professional footballer and what it's like working on the other side as one of the media.

In between the laughs, Aldo puts forward some controversial opinions about the big talking points dominating the game today.

From the infamous Thierry Henry handball that denied the Irish a World Cup place to the off-the-field issues that are threatening to tear Liverpool FC apart, Aldo gives his no-nonsense views.

It's a journey that you won't want to miss!

**Call 0845 143 0001 or visit www.merseyshop.com**

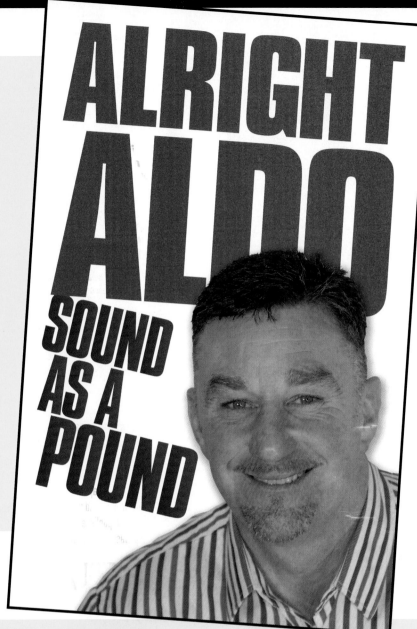

# Other offers and packages

Alan Hansen's Strangest Football Injuries - £4.50 plus £1.00 P&P (UK) - *Half Price*

Irish KOP - £8.50 plus £2.00 P&P (UK) - *Half Price*

Michael Shields - £2.50 plus £1.00 P&P (UK) - *Saving over £6.00*

Real Bob Paisley - £2.50 plus £3.50 P&P (UK) - *Saving over £17.00*

Phil Thompson Hardback - £2.50 plus £2.50 P&P (UK) - *Saving over £15.00*

Phil Thompson Paperback - £1.50 plus £1.00 P&P (UK) - *Saving over £7.00*

Play Like Liverpool - £5.00 plus £2.00 P&P (UK) - *Saving £10.00* - Available from 1st November 2010

Tops of the KOP - £4.50 plus £1.00 P&P (UK) - *Half Price*

### Packages

Dodgy Football Fashion and Alan Hansen - £12.50 plus £2.50 P&P (UK) - *Saving over £6.00*

LFC Guide 2011 and LFC Guide 2010 - £17.50, free P&P (UK) - *Saving over £10.00*

LFC Guide 2011 and LFC Songbook - £20.00, free P&P (UK)

*Please note: KOP10 discount does not apply on these offers and packages*

**Call 0845 143 0001 or visit www.merseyshop.com**

# THE KOP BOOK CLUB

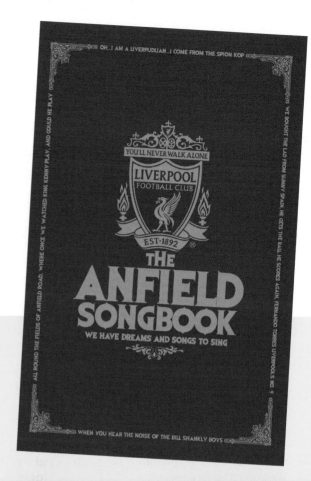

RRP: £9.99 **KOP₁₀** Price: £7.99

ANFIELD is a place of worship. And when it comes to inventing funny and inspirational songs for their team. No other set of fans can compare with the famous Kopites of Liverpool Football Club.

The Anfield Songbook is a collection of the timeless anthems, traditional classics, player chants and witty one-liners that have made the Kop unique.

From You'll Never Walk Alone to the Fernando Torres song, and from Liverbird Upon My Chest to Peter Crouch's feet sticking out of the bed....this book will fill you with pride and give you a laugh or two.

RRP: £8.99 **KOP₁₀** Price: £7.19

THIS official Liverpool FC Book is the perfect book to accompany a tour of the LFC Museum.

An insightful look into one of football's iconic stadiums and home of Liverpool Football Club. From inside the dressing room to out on the pitch, it has seen joy and despair; goals and glory; titles, tears and moments that pass in the twinkling of an eye, but last in the memory of a lifetime.

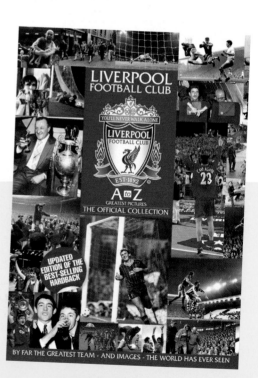

IMAGINE being given the keys to the vaults of Anfield Road and discovering the greatest photo album that any Liverpool fan could ask for. This incredible book is exactly that. From Liddell and Dalglish to Gerrard and Carragher. The heroes. The Legends. The forgotten men. The action. The tears. The laughter. The goals. The glory. The unexpected...

When it was first published in 2006 in hardback form, this book sold out. This new softback edition has been updated and revised to include some famous images from recent years, including some celebrated victories in Europe and the emergence of one of the world's leading strikers, Fernando Torres.

This official title captures the essence of what makes this great football club so special.

RRP: £12.99
**KOP₁₀** Price: £10.39

# Now sign up for a year of Kop laughs

If you like what you've read, why not subscribe to The Kop magazine every month of the year? We like taking the mick out of ourselves, but love having a laugh at our rivals' expense even more . . .

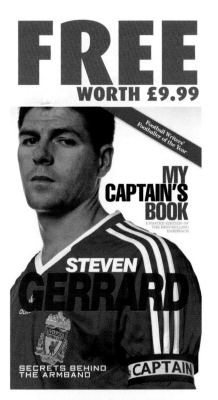

# FREE
## WORTH £9.99

**Get a FREE copy of STEVEN GERRARD MY CAPTAIN'S BOOK when you subscribe to The Kop Magazine. Simply quote KOPSG when ordering – NO JOKE!**

THE Kop Annual is just a flavour of what is produced every month in The Kop magazine.

So if you enjoy reading about the serious Anfield issues, but also love poking fun at the Mancs and falling about laughing at Everton's new away strip, why not sign up for a year's supply of The Kop?

Just call us on 0845 143 0001 or you can also visit merseyshop.com.

Or take a look at our yearly rates, fill in the form below and send it to Kop Subscriptions, Sport Media, PO Box 48, Old Hall Street, Liverpool L69 3EB.

Sign up for The Kop – it'll have you laughing more than the time you saw that flag aimed at Purslow on the Kop.